LOIRE FRANCE TRAVEL GUIDE 2025

THELMA JASON

Copyright © 2025 by Thelma Jason

All rights reserved. No part of this book may be copied, reproduced, distributed, or transmitted in any form or by any means without explicit written permission from the author or publisher. Under no circumstances shall the author or publisher be held liable for any damages, financial loss, or other consequences arising from the use or misuse of the information in this book.

Legal Notice
This book is protected under copyright law. It is intended for personal use only. You may not modify, distribute, sell, or quote any part of this book without prior consent from the author or publisher.

Disclaimer
The information in this book is provided for educational and entertainment purposes only. Every effort has been made to ensure the content is accurate, reliable, and up to date. However, no guarantees or warranties of any kind are implied.
Readers acknowledge that the author is not providing professional advice, whether legal, financial, medical, or otherwise. If you plan to apply any information from this book, please consult a licensed professional beforehand.

By reading this book, you agree that the author is not responsible for any direct or indirect losses resulting from errors, omissions, or inaccuracies in the content.

GET ACCESS TO MORE BOOKS BY THE AUTHOR

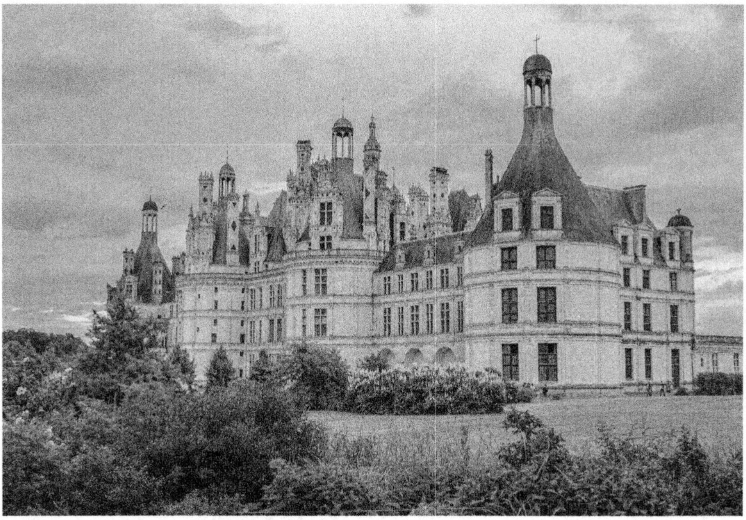

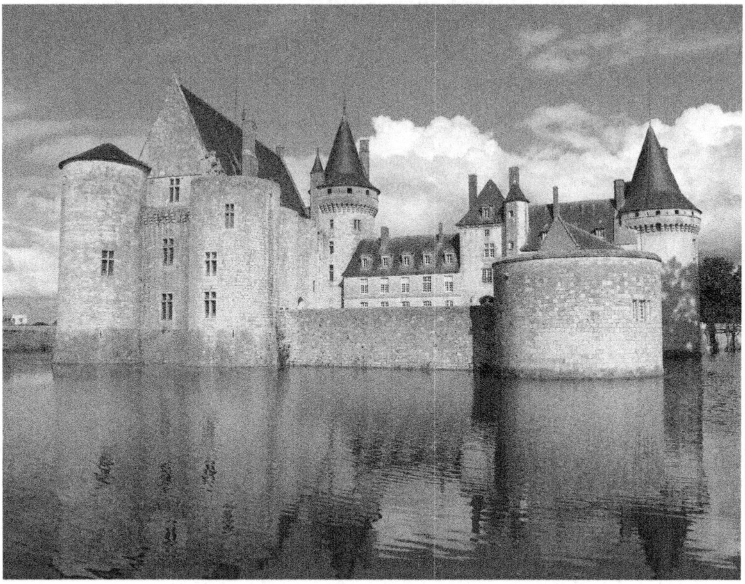

TABLE OF CONTENTS

CHAPTER 1: INTRODUCTION — 12
   Who This Guide Is For — 15
   Best Times to Visit the Loire Valley and Why — 17

CHAPTER 2: BEFORE YOU GO — 21
   Essential Travel Tips — 21
   Key French Phrases for the Loire Region — 25
   Packing Checklist for the Loire Valley — 29
   Accessories for Cycling Routes in the Loire Valley — 32

CHAPTER 3: TRAVEL LOGISTICS — 36
   How to Get to the Loire Valley — 36
   Tips for Renting a Car for Countryside Exploration in the Loire Valley — 40
   Best Apps for Navigating Rural Areas and Finding Local Events in the Loire Valley — 46

CHAPTER 4: TOP DESTINATIONS IN THE LOIRE VALLEY — 52
   Iconic Châteaux of the Loire Valley — 53
   Charming Towns of the Loire Valley — 58
   Hidden Gems of the Loire Valley — 63
   Forest Walks and Nature Escapes — 66

CHAPTER 5: WHAT TO DO IN THE LOIRE VALLEY — 68
   Outdoor Adventures in the Loire Valley — 69
   Wine & Gastronomy in the Loire Valley — 73
   Regional Specialties in the Loire Valley — 77

Suggested Local Markets and Eateries	79
Cultural Highlights of the Loire Valley	82

CHAPTER 6: PRACTICAL INFORMATION FOR THE LOIRE VALLEY — 87

Accommodation Options in the Loire Valley	92
Unique Stays: Troglodyte Lodgings and More	95
Budgeting for Your Trip to the Loire Valley	96

CHAPTER 7: SAMPLE ITINERARIES FOR THE LOIRE VALLEY — 101

3-Day Highlights Tour: Iconic Châteaux and Wine Tastings	102
5-Day Immersion: A Mix of Famous Spots and Lesser-Known Gems	105

CHAPTER 8: Seasonal Events & Festivals — 112

Spring: A Time for Renewal and Celebration	112
Summer: Festivals, Music, and Outdoor Fun	113
Autumn: Harvest Celebrations and Scenic Beauty	115
Year-Round Events: A Celebration of Loire's Heritage	116

CHAPTER 9: TRAVEL ETIQUETTE AND LOCAL INSIGHTS — 118

Respecting Historical Sites and Monuments	118
General Local Etiquette	121
Cultural Tips for Interacting with Locals in the Loire Valley	123

CHAPTER 10: FAQS AND TROUBLESHOOTING FOR THE LOIRE VALLEY — 129

What should I do in case of a medical emergency in the Loire Valley?	130

What should I do if I lose my passport or wallet?	131
What should I do if I have trouble with public transportation?	131
What should I do if there's bad weather during my visit?	132
What should I do if I don't speak French and have trouble communicating?	133
What should I do if I miss an event or activity I had planned?	134
How to Handle Language Barriers Effectively in the Loire Valley	135
FINAL WORDS	**141**

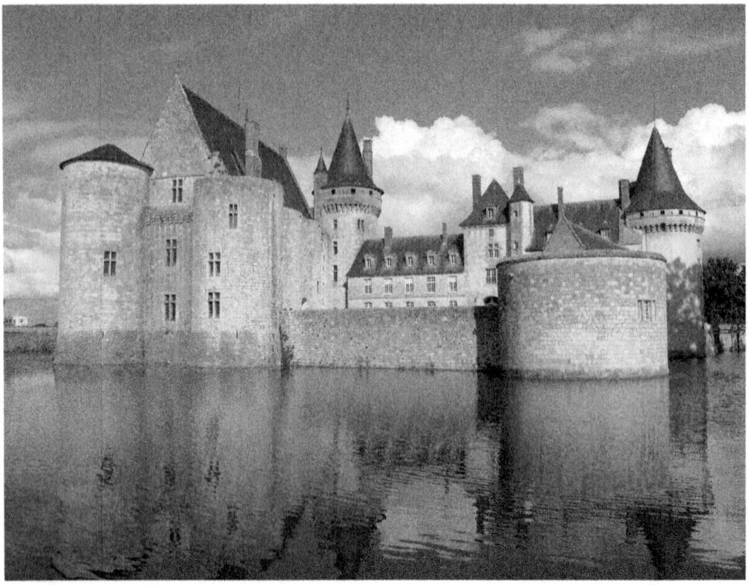

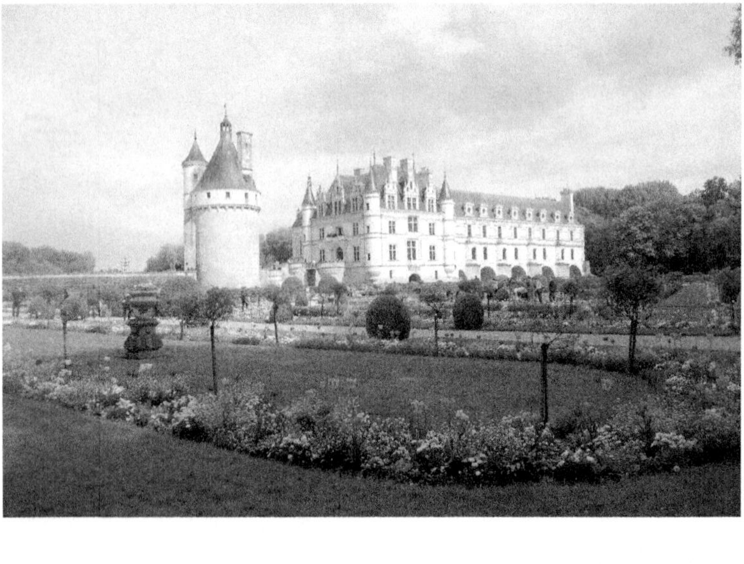

11

CHAPTER 1: INTRODUCTION

The Loire Valley, known as the "Garden of France," is one of the most enchanting regions in the country. Nestled in the heart of central France, this UNESCO World Heritage Site stretches along the majestic Loire River, offering visitors a perfect blend of history, culture, and natural beauty. Famous for its grand châteaux, picturesque vineyards, and tranquil riverscapes, the Loire is a place where time seems to slow down, inviting travelers to immerse themselves in its timeless charm.

A Region of Fairytale Châteaux

No visit to the Loire would be complete without exploring its iconic châteaux, which stand as proud reminders of France's royal and aristocratic past. These architectural masterpieces, ranging from medieval fortresses to Renaissance palaces, are dotted across the region, creating a landscape that feels straight out of a storybook. Château de Chambord, with its intricate design and sprawling grounds, epitomizes French Renaissance architecture, while Château de Chenonceau, elegantly spanning the River Cher, captures the romance and intrigue of its storied history.

But the allure of the Loire's châteaux extends beyond its most famous landmarks. Smaller, lesser-known gems like Château d'Azay-le-Rideau or Château de Villandry, with its meticulously designed gardens, offer intimate glimpses into the region's past. Whether you're marveling at the grandeur of Chambord or strolling through the fragrant rose gardens of a hidden estate, the châteaux are a window into a bygone era of opulence and artistry.

Rolling Vineyards and World-Class Wines

The Loire is also celebrated as one of France's most prestigious wine regions. With vineyards stretching as far as the eye can see, this is the place to indulge in some of the finest wines the country has to offer. From crisp Sancerres and vibrant Sauvignon Blancs to the rich reds of Chinon and delicate sparkling wines of Saumur, the Loire Valley's wine offerings are as diverse as its landscape.

A visit to the Loire isn't just about tasting the wines—it's about experiencing the culture that surrounds them. Many vineyards offer guided tours and tastings, allowing visitors to learn about the unique terroir, winemaking traditions, and passion that goes into every bottle. Pair your wine experience with local specialties, such as creamy goat cheese or tarte Tatin, for an authentic taste of the region.

Serene Riverscapes and Natural Beauty

At the heart of the Loire is its river, winding gracefully through the countryside and weaving together the region's châteaux, vineyards, and villages. The river has been the lifeblood of the Loire for centuries, shaping its landscapes and nurturing its fertile plains. Today, it offers a tranquil setting for travelers looking to escape the hustle of modern life.

Take a leisurely bike ride along the Loire à Vélo, a scenic cycling trail that follows the river and offers breathtaking views of the valley. Alternatively, hop aboard a traditional flat-bottomed boat for a peaceful cruise, where you can admire the châteaux and vineyards from the water. Nature lovers will also appreciate the region's diverse wildlife, from herons and kingfishers along the riverbanks to deer grazing in the nearby forests.

A Timeless Blend of Culture and Heritage

The Loire Valley isn't just about its landmarks—it's about the stories they tell and the way they connect you to the past. From medieval battles fought in its castles to the royal courts that once graced its halls, the region is steeped in history. Villages like Amboise, where Leonardo da Vinci spent his final years, and Tours, with its vibrant markets and half-timbered houses, are brimming with character and charm.

Throughout the year, the Loire comes alive with festivals and events that celebrate its rich heritage. From harvest celebrations in the vineyards to music and art festivals held in the shadow of its châteaux, there's always something happening to immerse you in the spirit of the region.

Why Visit the Loire Valley?

The Loire Valley offers something for every type of traveler. History buffs will revel in its ancient castles and historic towns. Foodies and wine enthusiasts will delight in its culinary and viticultural treasures. Nature lovers will find peace in its rolling hills and meandering rivers. Families, couples, and solo travelers alike will discover that the Loire is more than a destination—it's an experience that stays with you long after you've left.

This guide is your key to unlocking the magic of the Loire. Whether you're planning your first visit or returning to explore new corners, it will help you navigate the region's highlights and uncover its hidden gems. Prepare to be captivated by the beauty, culture, and charm of the Loire Valley—a place where every moment feels like a step into a dream.

Who This Guide Is For

The Loire Valley is a destination that caters to a diverse range of travelers, offering something special for everyone. Whether you're a connoisseur of fine wines, a history buff with a passion for ancient tales, or simply seeking a tranquil escape with your loved ones, the Loire has a way of leaving an indelible mark on its visitors.

Wine Lovers

If your heart beats for vineyards and vintages, the Loire Valley is your paradise. Known as one of France's premier wine regions, it's a haven for those who appreciate fine wines paired with stunning scenery. From the crisp whites of Sancerre to the sparkling wines of Saumur, this is your opportunity to savor the best the region has to offer. This guide will lead you to top vineyards, intimate wine tastings, and scenic wine routes that highlight the diversity and excellence of Loire Valley wines.

History Enthusiasts

For those fascinated by history, the Loire is a treasure trove of stories waiting to be uncovered. With over 300 châteaux, many dating back centuries, the region is often referred to as the "Valley of the Kings." Whether it's exploring the grand halls of Château de Chambord, tracing the footsteps of Leonardo da Vinci in Amboise, or delving into medieval tales in Chinon, this guide will help you delve into the rich historical tapestry of the Loire Valley.

Families

Traveling with children? The Loire Valley is perfect for families, offering activities that blend fun and learning. Explore kid-friendly châteaux with interactive exhibits, enjoy leisurely bike rides along the Loire à Vélo trails, or spend a day at one of the region's many zoos and adventure parks. This guide includes practical tips to make traveling with kids stress-free and memorable, ensuring everyone in the family has an enjoyable experience.

Romantic Travelers

Few places exude romance quite like the Loire Valley. Picture yourselves strolling hand-in-hand through fragrant château gardens, sharing a bottle of local wine as the sun sets over the river, or staying in a fairytale castle for the night. Whether you're planning a honeymoon, anniversary trip, or simply a romantic getaway, this guide will help you find the most intimate and enchanting spots to share with your loved one.

This guide is designed with your passions and interests in mind. Whether you're sipping wine in a sunlit vineyard, marveling at the grandeur of a historic château, or creating memories with your family, the Loire Valley offers an unforgettable journey for every traveler.

Best Times to Visit the Loire Valley and Why

The Loire Valley is a year-round destination, but each season brings its unique charm and experiences. Whether you're captivated by springtime blooms, the golden hues of autumn vineyards, or the lively atmosphere of summer festivals, the Loire offers something unforgettable no matter when you visit.

Spring (March to May): A Symphony of Blooms

Spring in the Loire Valley is a feast for the senses. The gardens of its famous châteaux burst into life with vibrant tulips, daffodils, and wisteria. Notable gardens like those at Château de Villandry and Château de Chenonceau are especially breathtaking during this season. The mild temperatures, averaging 10–20°C (50–68°F), make it perfect for exploring the countryside on foot or by bike.

Why Visit in Spring?

- Garden lovers' paradise: Ideal for strolling through meticulously landscaped château gardens.

- Fewer crowds: Enjoy iconic sites in a more relaxed atmosphere before the summer rush.

- Fresh local produce: Experience springtime flavors at farmers' markets, including asparagus, strawberries, and Loire wines.

Summer (June to August): Festivals and Long Days

Summer is peak tourist season, and for good reason. With warm temperatures ranging from 20–30°C (68–86°F), this is the time to enjoy outdoor activities, from kayaking on the Loire River to cycling along the Loire à Vélo routes. Festivals light up the season, such as the Son et Lumière (Sound and Light) shows at châteaux like Blois and Azay-le-Rideau, and the vibrant Les Heures Historiques in Sully-sur-Loire.

Why Visit in Summer?

- Festivals galore: Witness spectacular events and cultural celebrations.

- Extended daylight: Long days mean more time to explore the region's attractions.

- Outdoor adventures: Ideal for picnics, vineyard visits, and riverside strolls.

Autumn (September to November): A Golden Retreat

Autumn transforms the Loire Valley into a canvas of golden and amber hues. Vineyards come alive with the grape harvest, making it an excellent time to tour wineries and sample fresh vintages. Temperatures are cooler, averaging 10–20°C (50–68°F), providing a cozy yet crisp backdrop for exploring châteaux and forests.

Why Visit in Autumn?

- Harvest season: Immerse yourself in the wine culture with tastings and vineyard tours.

- Photographer's dream: Capture the stunning fall foliage across the valley.

- Tranquil ambiance: Fewer visitors make for a more serene experience.

Winter (December to February): A Quiet Escape

While winter may not showcase the Loire's famous gardens, it offers a peaceful charm. Many châteaux host festive events, including Christmas markets and holiday lights at places like Château de Chambord. With temperatures averaging 3–8°C (37–46°F), it's a cozy time for wine tasting in cellar caves or enjoying hearty French cuisine by the fire.

Why Visit in Winter?

• Festive magic: Celebrate the holidays in enchanting château settings.

• Lower prices: Take advantage of off-season rates on accommodations and attractions.

• Quiet beauty: Enjoy iconic landmarks without the crowds.

Choosing the Right Season for Your Visit

• For gardens and mild weather: Visit in spring.

• For festivals and lively atmosphere: Opt for summer.

• For wine and autumnal scenery: Plan your trip in autumn.

• For budget-friendly tranquility: Explore in winter.

Each season in the Loire Valley brings its own highlights, so the best time to visit depends on your interests and travel style.

CHAPTER 2: BEFORE YOU GO

2. Proper preparation ensures a seamless trip to the Loire Valley. From understanding travel requirements to packing the essentials, these tips will help you make the most of your adventure.

Essential Travel Tips

• Plan Your Itinerary: The Loire Valley spans a large area with numerous attractions, so prioritize the châteaux, vineyards, and towns you want to visit. Group nearby sites to minimize travel time.

• **Transport Options:**

- **By Car:** Renting a car is highly recommended for flexibility, especially if you plan to explore smaller towns and rural vineyards.

- **By Train:** The TGV connects Paris to cities like Tours and Angers in under two hours. Local trains and buses can help you reach other destinations.

- **By Bike:** The Loire à Vélo cycling route offers a scenic way to explore the region.

- **Book Accommodations Early:** Popular spots like Tours and Amboise can fill up quickly, especially during peak seasons. Consider staying in charming gîtes (holiday cottages) or bed-and-breakfasts for an authentic experience.

- **Pack Appropriately:**

  - Comfortable walking shoes for château tours and cobblestone streets.

  - Layered clothing to adapt to variable weather, especially in spring and autumn.

  - A reusable water bottle for long days of exploration.

Documents and Currency

- **Passport and Visa:**

  - If you're traveling from outside the European Union, ensure your passport is valid for at least six months beyond your travel dates.

- Visitors from the U.S., Canada, Australia, and other visa-exempt countries can stay in France for up to 90 days within a 180-day period.

- ETIAS Authorization: Starting in 2024, travelers from visa-exempt countries need an ETIAS (European Travel Information and Authorization System) approval to enter France. This can be completed online.

- **Driver's License:**

- If renting a car, bring your valid driver's license. Non-EU travelers may need an International Driving Permit (IDP). Check with your rental company for specific requirements.

- **Currency:**

- The official currency is the Euro (€). Credit and debit cards are widely accepted, but carrying some cash for smaller purchases or rural areas is advisable.

- ATMs are readily available in towns and cities. Use a bank-affiliated ATM to minimize fees.

- **Travel Insurance:**

- Consider comprehensive travel insurance that covers medical emergencies, trip cancellations, and lost belongings.

- EU travelers should bring their EHIC/GHIC card for access to healthcare.

Local Etiquette and Language Tips

- Basic French Phrases: While many locals in tourist areas speak English, learning a few French phrases like "Bonjour" (Hello), "Merci" (Thank you), and "Où est…?" (Where is…?) will enhance your experience.

- **Dining Etiquette:**

- Reserve tables in advance, especially for popular restaurants.

- Expect leisurely meals; rushing is uncommon in French dining culture.

- Tipping: Service charges are typically included, but leaving a small tip (5–10%) for exceptional service is appreciated.

Technology and Connectivity

- Adapters and Voltage: France uses Type C and E outlets with a 230V supply. Bring a universal adapter for your devices.

- SIM Cards and Data: If you need mobile data, consider purchasing a local SIM card or using an international roaming plan. Wi-Fi is widely available in hotels and cafés.

- Navigation: Download offline maps or a navigation app like Google Maps to help you get around.

By preparing thoroughly, you can focus on enjoying the Loire Valley's timeless beauty, rich culture, and unforgettable experiences. A little planning goes a long way!

Key French Phrases for the Loire Region

Having a few essential French phrases at your disposal will greatly enhance your experience in the Loire Valley, where smaller towns and rural areas may have fewer English speakers. Here's a list tailored to common scenarios you'll encounter in the region:

Greetings and Polite Expressions

- Bonjour ! – Hello (daytime)
- Bonsoir ! – Good evening
- Merci ! – Thank you
- S'il vous plaît. – Please
- Excusez-moi. – Excuse me
- Je suis désolé(e). – I'm sorry
- Au revoir. – Goodbye
- À bientôt ! – See you soon!

Asking for Directions

- Où est… ? – Where is…?
- le château ? – the château?
- la gare ? – the train station?

- le marché ? – the market?
- Pouvez-vous m'aider ? – Can you help me?
- C'est loin ? – Is it far?
- À gauche / À droite. – To the left / To the right.
- Tout droit. – Straight ahead.

Dining and Food

- Je voudrais… – I would like…
- un verre de vin blanc/rouge. – a glass of white/red wine.
- un café, s'il vous plaît. – a coffee, please.
- Avez-vous une table pour deux ? – Do you have a table for two?
- Quelle est la spécialité régionale ? – What is the local specialty?
- L'addition, s'il vous plaît. – The bill, please.
- C'est délicieux ! – It's delicious!

Shopping and Markets

- Combien ça coûte ? – How much does it cost?

- Pouvez-vous me montrer ça ? – Can you show me that?
- Je cherche… – I'm looking for…
- un souvenir. – a souvenir.
- un bon vin. – a good wine.
- Avez-vous des produits locaux ? – Do you have local products?

Châteaux and Sightseeing

- Quels sont les horaires d'ouverture ? – What are the opening hours?
- Faut-il réserver ? – Do I need to book in advance?
- Y a-t-il une visite guidée ? – Is there a guided tour?
- Puis-je prendre des photos ? – Can I take photos?

Emergency and Assistance

- Où sont les toilettes ? – Where are the restrooms?
- Aidez-moi, s'il vous plaît. – Please help me.
- Je suis perdu(e). – I'm lost.

- Appelez un taxi, s'il vous plaît. – Please call a taxi.

- Y a-t-il une pharmacie à proximité ? – Is there a pharmacy nearby?

- C'est une urgence. – It's an emergency.

Wine Tasting and Vineyards

- Puis-je goûter ce vin ? – Can I taste this wine?

- Quel vin recommandez-vous ? – Which wine do you recommend?

- Est-ce que ce vin est sec / doux ? – Is this wine dry / sweet?

- Je voudrais acheter une bouteille. – I would like to buy a bottle.

- Merci pour la dégustation ! – Thank you for the tasting!

Travel and Transport

- Un billet pour Tours, s'il vous plaît. – A ticket to Tours, please.

- À quelle heure part le prochain train ? – What time does the next train leave?

- Où se trouve l'arrêt de bus ? – Where is the bus stop?

- Pouvez-vous appeler un taxi ? – Can you call a taxi?

Mastering even a few of these phrases will help you navigate the Loire region with confidence and make meaningful connections with the locals. Don't worry about perfect pronunciation—most will appreciate your effort!

Packing Checklist for the Loire Valley

Preparing for your trip to the Loire Valley means packing with its diverse activities and temperate climate in mind. Here's a detailed checklist to ensure you're ready for château tours, vineyard visits, and scenic countryside strolls:

Clothing and Footwear

- Comfortable Walking Shoes: Essential for exploring expansive château grounds, cobbled streets, and picturesque villages. Opt for sturdy sneakers or lightweight hiking shoes.

- Layers for Varying Weather: The Loire Valley's climate can change quickly. Pack a mix of:

  - Light t-shirts or blouses for warmer days.

  - A sweater or fleece for cooler mornings and evenings.

  - A waterproof jacket or raincoat for unexpected showers, especially in spring and fall.

29

• Smart-Casual Attire: Bring something slightly dressier for dining at fine restaurants or attending wine tastings.

• Scarf or Shawl: Useful for layering and as a stylish accessory, especially during shoulder seasons.

Travel Essentials

• Daypack or Small Backpack: Handy for carrying water, snacks, and essentials during day trips.

• Reusable Water Bottle: Stay hydrated while exploring the region's vast landscapes. Many towns have public fountains with drinkable water.

• Sunglasses and Hat: Protect yourself from the sun during vineyard tours or summer visits.

• Travel Umbrella: Compact and lightweight, ideal for sudden rain.

Documents and Travel Accessories

• Valid Passport: Ensure it's up-to-date and has at least six months' validity remaining.

• Travel Insurance Details: Keep a printed copy of your policy for emergencies.

• Copies of Reservations: Print confirmations for accommodations, car rentals, and château entry tickets.

- Local Maps or Guidebook: Although GPS is helpful, a physical map or guidebook can be invaluable in rural areas with limited connectivity.

Tech and Electronics

- Universal Power Adapter: France uses Type C and Type E plugs with a voltage of 230V.

- Portable Charger: Keep your devices powered for navigation and photos.

- Camera or Smartphone with Storage: Capture the beauty of the Loire's castles, vineyards, and riverscapes.

- Earbuds or Headphones: Perfect for enjoying audio guides during tours.

Health and Personal Care

- Medications: Pack any prescriptions and a small first-aid kit with essentials like pain relievers, band-aids, and antihistamines.

- Sunscreen and Lip Balm: Protect your skin, especially during outdoor excursions.

- Insect Repellent: Useful during summer evenings or visits to gardens and vineyards.

- Toiletries: Hotels often provide basics, but pack your preferred items like toothpaste, shampoo, and deodorant.

Optional Items

- Notebook or Journal: Record your impressions, favorite wines, and travel memories.

- Binoculars: Great for spotting details in château architecture or enjoying views across the Loire River.

- Picnic Gear: A lightweight blanket and reusable utensils can be perfect for enjoying local produce by the river.

By packing these essentials, you'll be well-prepared to enjoy the Loire Valley's charm and beauty, no matter the season or itinerary.

Accessories for Cycling Routes in the Loire Valley

Cycling through the Loire Valley is one of the most scenic ways to explore this beautiful region, whether you're meandering through vineyards, visiting historical châteaux, or cycling along the peaceful Loire River. To ensure your ride is comfortable and enjoyable, here's a list of accessories to bring along for your cycling adventure:

Cycling Gear

- Helmet: Safety first! Whether you're renting a bike or bringing your own, a properly fitted helmet is essential, especially on longer or more challenging routes.

• Cycling Gloves: These help improve grip, reduce hand fatigue, and protect your palms from potential falls.

• Padded Shorts or Cycling Tights: Long hours in the saddle can be uncomfortable without proper padding. Opt for cycling shorts to avoid chafing on longer rides.

• Cycling Shoes: If you're serious about cycling, consider shoes with clips for better pedal efficiency, but comfortable sneakers work well for casual riders.

• Reflective Vest or Vest with LED Lights: If you plan to cycle in low-light conditions or at night, make sure you're visible to drivers and other cyclists.

• Cycling Jacket or Windbreaker: Weather in the Loire can change quickly, so bring a lightweight, packable jacket to protect you from wind and rain. A breathable, waterproof jacket is a good choice for comfort.

Bike Accessories

• Water Bottle and Holder: Hydration is key! A water bottle holder mounted on your bike frame makes it easy to stay refreshed while cycling.

• Bike Lock: A compact, reliable lock is essential when stopping at local markets, cafés, or châteaux.

•   Repair Kit: Accidents happen, and it's important to be prepared. A small kit with spare tubes, tire levers, a pump, and a multi-tool can help you fix minor issues on the go.

•   Front and Rear Lights: If you're cycling at dusk or dawn, bike lights are essential for visibility and safety.

•   Saddle Bag or Panniers: A small bag under your seat or panniers attached to your bike will hold essential items like your phone, map, snacks, or camera without weighing you down.

•   GPS or Cycling Map: Having a bike-specific map or GPS device can help you stay on track. Many bike routes are well-marked, but having a backup for longer rides is always wise.

Comfort and Convenience

•   Sunscreen: Cycling in the open air means more exposure to the sun. Apply sunscreen before you head out and bring it with you for reapplication during longer rides.

•   Lip Balm with SPF: Protect your lips from the sun, especially when cycling through exposed vineyards or along the river.

•   Snacks and Energy Bars: Long cycling routes can burn through your energy. Pack some quick snacks like energy bars, dried fruit, or nuts for a boost on the go.

- Hand Sanitizer or Wipes: Keep your hands clean during stops or after handling your bike.

- Earphones: If you enjoy listening to music or podcasts during your ride, consider bringing lightweight earphones (but always keep your surroundings in mind for safety).

For Longer Rides or Multi-Day Cycling Trips

- Cycling Backpack: If you plan to cycle for multiple days, a comfortable backpack or hydration pack will help carry your essentials like extra clothes, snacks, or a camera.

- Portable Charger: For longer rides, keep a portable charger to ensure your phone or GPS remains powered, especially if you're using it for navigation or photos.

- Extra Clothing Layers: Bring additional layers if you're cycling in the cooler months or tackling longer rides. A lightweight fleece or vest can be easily packed into a backpack or panniers.

Cycling the Loire Valley is an unforgettable experience, offering stunning views of the countryside, rivers, and iconic landmarks. By bringing the right accessories, you'll ensure your ride is comfortable, safe, and memorable. Whether you're on a leisurely tour or tackling a multi-day cycling route, these items will help you make the most of your adventure.

CHAPTER 3: TRAVEL LOGISTICS

How to Get to the Loire Valley

The Loire Valley, with its picturesque châteaux, rolling vineyards, and charming villages, is easily accessible from several transportation hubs. Whether you're arriving from Paris, other major French cities, or even nearby countries, there are a number of options for getting to this beautiful region. Here's a breakdown of your travel options to make planning your trip to the Loire Valley simple and straightforward.

1. By Train

The train system in France is efficient, fast, and convenient, making it one of the best ways to travel to the Loire Valley.

- TGV (High-Speed Train) from Paris: The most popular and efficient way to reach the Loire is by taking the TGV (Train à Grande Vitesse), France's high-speed train service. From Paris Gare Montparnasse, you can catch a direct TGV to several cities in the Loire Valley, including Tours, Orléans, Angers, and Blois. The journey typically takes about 1.5 to 2 hours depending on your destination. TGV trains are comfortable and offer onboard services, including Wi-Fi on some routes.

- Regional Trains (TER): For more specific destinations or to reach smaller towns, you can also take a TER (Train Express Régional), which connects various parts of the Loire Valley with major cities. While the journey may take a little longer than the TGV, it is still a great way to travel through the region.

- Booking Tickets: You can book your train tickets via the official French rail website SNCF or through other online platforms like Trainline. It's recommended to book in advance, especially if you're traveling during peak seasons, as the trains can fill up quickly.

2. By Car

Renting a car provides flexibility and is an excellent way to explore the Loire Valley, especially if you want to visit multiple châteaux, vineyards, or quaint villages at your own pace.

- Driving from Paris: The Loire Valley is about a 2.5 to 3-hour drive from Paris, depending on where you're headed. The most common route is to take the A10 motorway, which leads directly to major cities like Tours,

Blois, and Amboise. The road is well-maintained and offers scenic views of the countryside as you approach the valley.

• Car Rental: If you're not already in France, you can rent a car from Paris or other major cities. Rental agencies are available at Paris Charles de Gaulle Airport and in most cities throughout the country. Be sure to check rental conditions, especially regarding driving distances and fuel charges. If you plan on visiting rural areas or smaller villages, a car is highly recommended.

• Parking: While driving offers flexibility, it's important to know that parking in some of the smaller towns can be limited or costly. Many towns offer parking areas outside the center, so make sure to plan accordingly.

3. By Air

For those traveling from abroad or other parts of France, flying into one of the Loire Valley's nearby airports is a viable option.

• Tours Val de Loire Airport (TUF): Located just outside of Tours, this is the region's primary airport. It serves a number of European destinations and offers flights from cities like London, Dublin, and Amsterdam. From the airport, you can easily rent a car or take a shuttle to explore the Loire Valley.

• Nantes Atlantique Airport (NTE): Located around 2 hours west of the Loire Valley, Nantes' airport is another good option, with flights coming in from various European cities. It's a bit farther away from the châteaux, but still a viable option if you're traveling from northern Europe.

• Paris Airports (Charles de Gaulle or Orly): If you're coming from a major international destination, flying into Paris may be your best bet. From there, you can take a TGV train directly to the Loire or rent a car and drive, as Paris is just a short distance away.

4. By Bus

If you're on a budget, buses can be an affordable option, although they are slower than trains and cars.

• FlixBus and Ouibus: These services run long-distance routes across France, including to the Loire Valley. You can take a bus from Paris to cities like Tours, Orléans, and Angers. The journey may take a few hours longer than the train, but it's typically cheaper, especially if you book in advance.

• Local Bus Routes: Once you're in the Loire Valley, regional bus services can help you get from one city to another. However, bus routes may not be as frequent or convenient for exploring the châteaux, so a car rental is often more practical for exploring smaller towns.

5. Getting Around the Loire Valley

Once you've arrived in the Loire Valley, there are several options for getting around:

• Bicycle Rentals: Cycling is a fantastic way to explore the Loire Valley, especially if you're visiting the vineyards, countryside, and smaller villages. Many towns offer bike rentals, and there are several established bike routes throughout the region.

• Public Transport: The Loire Valley is served by buses and local trains, but these services are less frequent than in larger cities. If you're staying in major towns like Tours or Angers, you'll have more options for getting around, but if you're exploring rural areas or châteaux, a car rental is more practical.

• Guided Tours: If you prefer not to drive, many companies offer guided tours of the Loire Valley, including châteaux visits, wine-tasting tours, and cycling excursions. These can be a good option if you're short on time or want a hassle-free experience.

With these travel logistics in mind, getting to and around the Loire Valley is a straightforward process. Whether you prefer the speed of the train, the flexibility of driving, or the ease of flying into nearby airports, you'll find plenty of options to suit your needs and travel style. So, get ready to embark on your journey to one of France's most beautiful regions!

Tips for Renting a Car for Countryside Exploration in the Loire Valley

Renting a car is one of the best ways to explore the Loire Valley's picturesque countryside, charming villages, and iconic châteaux. However, driving in rural France can be a bit different from city driving, so here are some practical tips to make your experience smoother and more enjoyable.

1. Book in Advance

Especially during peak tourist seasons (spring to early autumn), renting a car in advance ensures better availability, lower rates, and a wider choice of vehicles. Booking online is quick, and many agencies offer flexible cancellation policies.

•   Where to Book: Consider booking through major rental companies like Europcar, Hertz, or Avis, or aggregator sites such as Rentalcars.com and Auto Europe.

•   Pick-up Location: You can pick up your rental car at airports, major train stations (like Tours or Nantes), or city centers.

2. Choose the Right Vehicle

When exploring the Loire Valley's countryside, a vehicle that suits both the rural terrain and your travel needs is important. Here are some considerations:

•   Compact Cars: The roads in the Loire Valley's cities and villages can be narrow, so a small or compact car may be ideal for maneuvering through tight spaces. They're also easier to park.

•   SUVs: If you plan to explore areas with rougher terrain or visit some of the more remote châteaux, an SUV may offer a more comfortable ride, especially in rural areas with less paved roads.

- Manual vs. Automatic: Manual transmission cars are more common in France, and they tend to be cheaper to rent. However, if you're not comfortable with a manual, ensure you book an automatic in advance. Be aware that automatic cars may have limited availability in rural locations.

3. Check the Rental Car's Condition

Before driving off, take a moment to inspect the car for any damage. Document any scratches, dents, or issues with the vehicle and report them to the rental company to avoid being charged later. Take photos for your own records.

- Fuel Type: Confirm whether the car uses gasoline or diesel, and check the fuel level at pick-up and drop-off.

- GPS or Maps: Ensure the vehicle has a GPS or navigation system, or plan ahead with offline maps on your phone (apps like Maps.me or Google Maps are useful in rural areas where signal may be weak).

4. Be Prepared for Narrow Roads

While the Loire Valley is known for its wide, scenic roads, many rural areas have narrow, winding country lanes, especially when approaching small villages or châteaux.

- Driving Etiquette: Stay alert and yield to oncoming traffic when necessary. If you're driving on narrow country roads, be courteous and give way to larger vehicles, especially farm trucks or delivery vehicles.

- Parking: Many towns and châteaux offer free or affordable parking, but spaces can be tight. Look for designated parking areas on the outskirts of popular attractions, and always park in clearly marked spaces to avoid fines.

5. Driving Laws to Keep in Mind

As with driving anywhere in France, there are a few important rules to follow:

- Speed Limits: In rural areas, the speed limit is typically 80 km/h (50 mph) on secondary roads and 130 km/h (81 mph) on highways (reducing to 110 km/h (68 mph) in wet weather). Always check for posted signs, as speed limits may vary.

- Seat Belts: Seat belts are required for all passengers in the car.

- Alcohol Limits: France has strict laws regarding drinking and driving. The legal blood alcohol limit is 0.05%, which is lower than many other countries. It's best not to drink at all if you plan to drive.

- Use of Phone: Using a mobile phone while driving is illegal unless you have a hands-free system.

6. Navigating the Loire Valley's Châteaux

Many of the Loire Valley's most famous châteaux are spread out across the region, and while they're generally well-signposted, the countryside roads can be confusing for first-time visitors.

- **Château Tours:** Plan your route in advance, and always check if the châteaux offer guided tours, as many have specific visiting hours.

- **Parking at Châteaux:** Most châteaux offer free parking or a small fee for parking in dedicated lots. At busy sites, arrive early or later in the day to avoid crowds and secure a good parking spot.

7. Prepare for Tolls and Road Charges

Driving in France means encountering toll roads (péages) on highways. These are common on routes from major cities like Paris to the Loire Valley.

- **Toll Costs:** The cost of tolls can add up, especially if you're traveling from Paris to the Loire Valley, where the tolls can be around €15-€20. Be sure to keep some cash or a credit card handy to pay the tolls.

- **Toll-Free Routes:** If you want to save on tolls, you can opt for scenic routes. These roads may take longer but offer a more leisurely and picturesque drive through the French countryside.

8. Be Mindful of the French Gas Stations

Fuel stations are available across the Loire Valley, but in more remote areas, they may be less frequent. Be sure to fill up when you pass a station to avoid running low in rural areas.

- **Paying for Fuel:** Many rural stations are self-service, especially after hours, so ensure you have a credit card or cash ready for payment. Some stations may also have fuel in diesel and petrol varieties, so be sure to select the correct one.

9. Returning the Car

When your journey in the Loire Valley comes to an end, you'll need to return your rental car. Be sure to refuel the car before dropping it off, as many rental agencies will charge an exorbitant fee for filling up the tank.

• Drop-off Locations: Most agencies offer drop-off at a variety of locations, including airports, city centers, and train stations. Be sure to check the rental company's policy to avoid extra fees.

• Inspect the Car Again: Once you return the car, ask for an inspection and confirm the return process.

10. Alternative: Renting a Car with Driver

If you'd rather not drive but still want to explore the Loire Valley at your own pace, consider renting a car with a driver or booking private tours. This can be especially convenient for wine tours or visits to multiple châteaux, as your driver will handle navigation and parking, allowing you to relax and enjoy the experience.

By following these tips, renting a car to explore the Loire Valley's stunning landscapes, vineyards, and historic sites will be a smooth and memorable experience. Whether you're traveling along scenic vineyard routes or exploring off-the-beaten-path villages, a car will give you the freedom to discover all that this incredible region has to offer.

Best Apps for Navigating Rural Areas and Finding Local Events in the Loire Valley

When traveling through the beautiful but sometimes remote Loire Valley, having the right apps can make your journey much easier and more enjoyable. From navigating winding rural roads to discovering local events and attractions, these apps are indispensable tools to help you get the most out of your trip.

1. Google Maps

Best for: General navigation, directions, and real-time traffic updates

Google Maps remains one of the most reliable and versatile navigation apps, especially when traveling in rural areas. It provides turn-by-turn directions, real-time traffic information, and detailed street maps. Even in rural areas of the Loire Valley, Google Maps works well for both driving and walking, helping you find your way to small towns, châteaux, vineyards, and hidden gems.

- Offline Maps: One of the app's standout features is the ability to download maps for offline use. This is especially helpful in rural areas with spotty cellular service.

• Street View: Google's Street View feature allows you to explore locations virtually before you visit, helping you prepare for your journey.

• Event Search: While not primarily for events, Google Maps can also highlight nearby events and attractions, like festivals or exhibitions, by searching for specific keywords (e.g., "wine festival" or "local concert").

2. Maps.me

Best for: Offline navigation and hiking routes

If you're traveling in remote parts of the Loire Valley where internet connectivity might be weak, Maps.me is an excellent choice. The app allows you to download detailed offline maps for free, which are especially helpful when navigating through rural areas or forests that lack cell coverage.

• Offline Functionality: Maps.me is great for navigating rural and less-traveled areas since the maps can be downloaded in advance and used without an internet connection.

• Tourist-Friendly Features: Maps.me includes information on attractions, hiking routes, historical sites, and more, making it perfect for exploring the Loire Valley's countryside.

3. Komoot

Best for: Outdoor activities, hiking, and cycling routes

For those interested in cycling or hiking through the Loire Valley's scenic routes, Komoot is the perfect app to plan your adventures. The app provides detailed trail maps, route planning, and elevation profiles for outdoor activities.

- Customized Routes: Komoot can help you tailor hiking and biking routes to your fitness level, duration preferences, and difficulty.

- Offline Maps: Just like Maps.me, you can download routes to use offline while you're exploring remote rural areas.

- Event Listings: The app often highlights local cycling events, outdoor meetups, and challenges happening in the region.

4. Eventbrite

Best for: Finding local events, festivals, and activities

If you're looking to immerse yourself in local culture and experience events during your stay in the Loire Valley, Eventbrite is one of the best apps to find festivals, performances, and other happenings.

- Local Events: Whether you're searching for wine festivals, local music performances, art exhibitions, or food markets, Eventbrite lists a wide range of events happening in cities and towns throughout the Loire Valley.

- Ticketing: If you find an event you like, you can also use Eventbrite to purchase tickets directly through the app.

- Personalized Recommendations: The app suggests events based on your location and interests, so you'll never miss out on something exciting.

5. TripAdvisor

Best for: Restaurant recommendations, tourist attractions, and reviews

For practical travel information and recommendations, TripAdvisor is an invaluable resource. Whether you're looking for the best local restaurants, must-see châteaux, or things to do in a specific town, TripAdvisor compiles reviews and recommendations from fellow travelers.

- Local Attractions: You can easily search for nearby landmarks, châteaux, and tourist attractions, complete with detailed descriptions, photos, and reviews.

- Local Events: TripAdvisor often lists local events, festivals, and seasonal activities, so you can stay up-to-date with what's happening in the Loire Valley while you're there.

- Dining Options: TripAdvisor provides reviews for restaurants, cafés, and wineries, so you can find the best places to eat as you explore the region.

6. Viator

Best for: Booking guided tours and local experiences

If you're interested in joining guided tours, local activities, or day trips in the Loire Valley, Viator is the app to use. It offers a wide selection of pre-booked tours, ranging from château visits to wine tastings and local sightseeing.

• Book Tours on the Go: Viator makes it easy to browse and book tours from local providers, helping you make the most of your time in the region.

• Local Experiences: Find experiences like cooking classes, wine tours, or private vineyard tastings, ideal for diving deeper into the local culture.

• User Reviews: Viator's reviews and ratings ensure that you can trust the quality of the tours and activities you book.

7. TheFork (LaFourchette)

Best for: Finding restaurants and making reservations

For foodies, TheFork (known as LaFourchette in France) is the app to have. It helps you find local restaurants, cafés, and bistros with user ratings, menus, and the ability to make reservations directly through the app.

• Restaurant Search: Search for dining options by location, cuisine, price range, or type of meal.

• Reservations: Book your table easily through TheFork, and even access special offers or discounts at selected restaurants.

• Local Recommendations: The app often highlights local food festivals, special events, or unique dining experiences, which are perfect for exploring the Loire Valley's culinary culture.

8. La Balade de l'Oiseau Blanc

Best for: Discovering off-the-beaten-path events and attractions

For those looking to discover unique, hidden events or attractions in the Loire Valley, La Balade de l'Oiseau Blanc is a niche app. It focuses on promoting off-the-beaten-path experiences, from boutique festivals to small, local markets.

• Hidden Gems: Find lesser-known events and unique attractions in the Loire Valley that may not be listed in larger travel guides.

• Interactive Features: The app provides interactive maps and detailed descriptions of local spots that may not be easily found elsewhere.

By using these apps, you'll be well-equipped to navigate rural areas in the Loire Valley, whether you're driving through picturesque towns, hiking or cycling along scenic routes, or immersing yourself in local events. These tools will enhance your travel experience, helping you uncover hidden gems and stay on top of the region's vibrant cultural happenings.

CHAPTER 4: TOP DESTINATIONS IN THE LOIRE VALLEY

The Loire Valley, often referred to as the "Garden of France," is a region brimming with stunning landscapes, historic towns, and, of course, its legendary châteaux. These castles, many of which date back to the Renaissance, are among the most iconic landmarks in France. Below are some of the top destinations in the Loire, each offering a unique glimpse into the region's rich history, culture, and architecture.

Iconic Châteaux of the Loire Valley

The Loire Valley is home to more than 300 châteaux, ranging from grand Renaissance palaces to medieval fortresses. These majestic structures, often surrounded by lush gardens and scenic riverscapes, reflect the area's significance during the French Renaissance and beyond. Let's explore some of the most iconic châteaux that you cannot miss during your visit to the Loire.

Château de Chambord: Renaissance Grandeur and Expansive Grounds

The Château de Chambord is perhaps the most famous and recognizable of all the Loire Valley châteaux. Known for its striking French Renaissance architecture, Chambord is a symbol of royal ambition, with its distinctive silhouette featuring a blend of medieval and classical influences. The château's creation was ordered by King François I in the early 16th century as a hunting lodge, and it has since become a masterpiece of design.

- Architectural Marvel: The château is famed for its double-helix staircase, designed by Leonardo da Vinci, and its massive roof, adorned with turrets and chimneys that resemble a fairytale castle. The symmetry of the design, coupled with the grandeur of its proportions, makes Chambord a sight to behold.

- Expansive Grounds: The château is set within a sprawling 13,000-acre park, making it one of the largest enclosed parks in Europe. It's perfect for a leisurely stroll or a bike ride through the picturesque woods and meadows, where you may catch glimpses of wildlife.

- Interior: Inside, the château boasts magnificent rooms, including the royal chambers, hunting lodges, and ornate galleries. The château's history and grandeur are showcased through exhibitions, giving visitors a glimpse into its past as a royal residence.

Visiting the Château de Chambord offers not just a look into Renaissance history but a truly immersive experience with its magnificent architecture and stunning natural surroundings. Whether you choose to explore the château on foot, bike, or even on horseback, Chambord is a place where history, nature, and art come together beautifully.

Château de Chenonceau: The Ladies' Château

One of the most elegant and romantic châteaux in the Loire Valley, Château de Chenonceau spans the River Cher, creating a breathtaking sight. Known as "The Ladies' Château" due to its association with several powerful women in history, this château is a must-see for its stunning beauty, rich history, and exceptional gardens.

- Historic Significance: The château was originally built in the 16th century and has had a fascinating history, from its ownership by King Henry II to its use as a hospital during World War I. It has been significantly shaped by the influence of women like Diane de Poitiers, who constructed the famous bridge across the river, and Catherine de Medici, who expanded and beautified the château.

- Architectural Beauty: The château's classic Renaissance style is combined with unique features, such as the bridge that crosses the Cher River, creating an almost surreal appearance. The interior showcases luxurious rooms, including the Queen's bedroom and the King's apartments, decorated with tapestries and period furnishings.

- Stunning Gardens: The château is renowned for its beautiful gardens, which are divided into distinct sections, including a formal garden, a vegetable garden, and an idyllic flower garden. The gardens are meticulously maintained and offer a serene and picturesque atmosphere perfect for leisurely strolls.

Château de Chenonceau stands as a symbol of beauty, grace, and power and provides an unforgettable experience for anyone visiting the Loire Valley.

Château de Villandry: The Gardens of Harmony

If you're a lover of gardens, Château de Villandry is one of the most enchanting destinations in the Loire Valley. This Renaissance château is known for its extraordinary and beautifully landscaped gardens, which are considered some of the most exquisite in all of France.

- Architectural Beauty: Villandry's design is classical, with an emphasis on symmetry and proportion, reflecting the Renaissance ideals of harmony. The château is less ornate on the inside than some of the other Loire châteaux, but it makes up for it with the grandeur of its gardens.

- Gardens: The highlight of Villandry is undoubtedly its gardens, designed by Jean Le Breton in the 16th century. The formal gardens are divided into distinct sections, including a water garden, a vegetable garden, and ornamental gardens featuring intricate flower patterns and geometrical designs. The gardens are so carefully designed that they are considered a perfect example of the Renaissance ideal of "garden as art."

- Seasonal Visits: Each season at Villandry brings a different experience. Spring and summer are ideal for seeing the flowers and vegetables in full bloom, while autumn offers a stunning display of harvest colors.

A visit to Château de Villandry is a true celebration of beauty and symmetry, offering a calm escape into the world of Renaissance garden design.

Château d'Azay-le-Rideau: A Gem of the Loire

The Château d'Azay-le-Rideau is often described as one of the most beautiful and romantic châteaux in the Loire Valley. Set on an island in the Indre River, it is renowned for its fairy-tale setting and exquisite Renaissance architecture.

- Architectural Charm: Built in the early 16th century, the château is known for its distinctive mix of French Renaissance and medieval styles. Its graceful towers and reflections in the river create a picture-perfect scene, making it one of the most photographed châteaux in the region.

• Interior: Inside, the château boasts splendid furnishings and art that reflect the opulence of the Renaissance period. Visitors can explore the rooms, which are furnished with antiques, tapestries, and paintings from the time of its construction.

• Château Gardens: The surrounding gardens, designed in the classic French style, offer a tranquil setting to explore. Whether walking through the manicured hedges or enjoying the peaceful riverside setting, Azay-le-Rideau offers a serene and picturesque experience.

A visit to Château d'Azay-le-Rideau is a journey into the elegance of Renaissance France, with the added charm of a beautiful riverside setting.

Château de Blois: A Royal Residence Through the Ages

The Château de Blois is one of the Loire Valley's most historically significant castles, as it was the residence of several French kings, including Louis XII and François I. Its architectural style reflects its long history, showcasing a mix of Gothic, Renaissance, and Classical elements.

• Historical Significance: Blois played a central role in French history, serving as a royal court during the 15th and 16th centuries. The château was the scene of dramatic events, including the assassination of the Duke of Guise in the 16th century.

• Distinct Architecture: The château's design is a fascinating blend of different architectural styles, from the medieval fortress to the elegant Renaissance wing. The royal apartments, grand staircases, and courtyards are perfect for history enthusiasts and architecture lovers alike.

- Interior and Exhibitions: Inside, the château houses a museum with exhibits on French royalty, providing insights into the life and times of the French kings and queens who lived there.

Château de Blois offers visitors an opportunity to step back in time, exploring a castle that played a pivotal role in the history of France.

Conclusion: Discovering the Heart of the Loire Valley

These are just a few of the iconic châteaux in the Loire Valley, each offering a unique experience that combines history, art, and stunning architecture. Whether you're interested in Renaissance grandeur, romantic settings, or lush gardens, the Loire Valley's châteaux provide an unforgettable journey through the heart of France's history.

Charming Towns of the Loire Valley

Beyond the iconic châteaux, the Loire Valley is home to picturesque towns and villages, each with its own unique character and charm. These towns, nestled along the river or hidden in the rolling hills, offer a delightful mix of history, culture, and local flavors. Whether you're drawn to vibrant markets, gastronomic experiences, or tranquil riverside walks, these charming towns provide the perfect complement to your Loire Valley adventure.

Tours: The Heart of the Loire Valley

Known as the "Gateway to the Loire Valley," Tours is a vibrant and historically rich city that beautifully captures the essence of the region. Situated on the banks of the Loire River, Tours is a perfect blend of modern life and medieval charm. It is often considered the heart of the Loire, offering a wide range of experiences that will appeal to food lovers, history buffs, and those seeking a taste of authentic French culture.

• Gastronomy and Markets: Tours is renowned for its culinary scene, with a strong focus on local products, fresh ingredients, and regional specialties. The city's markets, such as the Place des Halles market, are a must-visit for food lovers. Here, you'll find a vibrant array of fresh produce, local cheeses, wines, and pâtisseries. Make sure to try rillettes, a regional specialty of pork spread, or indulge in a tarte Tatin, the famous upside-down apple tart.

• Old Town Charm: The old town of Tours, with its narrow cobbled streets and medieval architecture, is a delightful place to explore. Wander through the Place Plumereau, a lively square lined with half-timbered houses and cafés, perfect for enjoying a coffee or aperitif. The Cathédrale Saint-Gatien, with its impressive Gothic facade and stunning stained-glass windows, is another highlight, offering a glimpse into the city's rich religious history.

• Cultural Heritage: Tours is also home to a variety of museums, such as the Musée des Beaux-Arts, which showcases an impressive collection of European art, or the Musée du Compagnonnage, which explores the traditional crafts and skills passed down through generations in the region. These museums offer insights into the history and culture of the Loire Valley, making them essential stops for those looking to deepen their understanding of the region.

- Riverfront Strolls: The Loire River runs through Tours, providing a serene backdrop for leisurely walks. The Promenade de Loire along the riverbank is a beautiful place to take in the views, enjoy the local flora, and watch the boats drift by. If you're feeling adventurous, consider taking a boat trip along the river to experience the Loire from a different perspective.

Amboise: Royal Heritage and Riverside Beauty

Just a short drive from Tours, Amboise is a small yet captivating town with a rich royal heritage. Situated along the Loire River, Amboise is famous for its stunning château, which once served as the residence of French kings and queens.

- Château d'Amboise: The crowning jewel of Amboise is the Château d'Amboise, a magnificent royal residence perched high above the town. This château is deeply tied to the history of the Renaissance, having been home to King Charles VIII and King François I, and is the final resting place of the great Leonardo da Vinci. The château's beautiful gardens and panoramic views of the Loire make it a must-visit.

- Charming Streets: Amboise's narrow streets are a delight to explore. With its Renaissance architecture, quaint shops, and lively cafés, the town exudes a peaceful atmosphere. Take a stroll through the old town, visit local artisan boutiques, or enjoy a meal at one of the many bistros that line the streets.

• Local Flavors: Amboise is also known for its excellent wines and fine dining. Visit one of the many wine bars to sample Vouvray or Chinon, two of the region's most famous wines. The Marché d'Amboise, held on Wednesdays and Sundays, is another highlight for food lovers, offering an assortment of fresh produce, cheeses, and meats.

Blois: A Town of Kings and Culture

With its rich history and royal ties, Blois is another charming town in the Loire Valley that offers a wealth of cultural experiences. Located along the Loire River, Blois served as the residence of several French kings, making it a key location during the Renaissance.

• Château de Blois: The town is home to the magnificent Château de Blois, which played an important role in the French monarchy. The château features a mix of medieval, Renaissance, and Classical architecture, reflecting the town's royal history. The Royal Apartments within the château offer a glimpse into the luxurious lives of French royalty, while the Maison de la Magie, a museum dedicated to magic and illusion, adds a quirky touch to your visit.

• Medieval Town Center: Blois' town center is a mix of old-world charm and vibrant modern life. Stroll through the Place du Château, a lively square with cafés, boutiques, and restaurants. Wander through the Rue de l'Embourie, a narrow street lined with medieval houses, and enjoy the atmosphere of this historic town.

• Cultural Experiences: Blois is also known for its festivals and cultural events. The Festival de la Magie is held every year, celebrating the art of magic, while Les Rendez-vous de l'Histoire brings together historians and enthusiasts for discussions and exhibitions. For art lovers, the Musée des Beaux-Arts de Blois is a must-visit, showcasing works from the Renaissance to modern times.

Saumur: The Town of Horses and Wine

Located on the banks of the Loire, Saumur is a town known for its equestrian heritage and exquisite wine production. The town is a hub for both horse enthusiasts and wine lovers, offering a unique blend of activities and experiences.

• Saumur Château: The Château de Saumur is a striking fortress that overlooks the town and the Loire River. Built in the 10th century, the château has served as a royal residence, a military stronghold, and even a prison. Today, it houses the Musée des Arts Décoratifs, showcasing a collection of historical artifacts and decorative arts.

• Equestrian Heritage: Saumur is home to the Cadre Noir, the prestigious French National Riding School, where visitors can watch impressive equestrian performances or take a tour of the stables. The town hosts equestrian events throughout the year, making it a great destination for horse lovers.

- Wine and Vineyards: The Saumur region is also renowned for its wines, particularly its Saumur-Champigny red wines and sparkling Crémant de Loire. Visit local wineries to sample the area's wines, or explore the Caves de Saumur, where wine is aged in the cool, underground cellars of the château.

The Loire Valley is full of charming towns that offer visitors a mix of history, culture, and natural beauty. Whether you're exploring the royal heritage of Tours, the romantic riverside charm of Amboise, or the cultural richness of Blois, each town has something unique to offer. With its exceptional gastronomy, picturesque streets, and welcoming atmosphere, the Loire Valley's towns are the perfect destinations for travelers seeking a blend of history, culture, and French joie de vivre.

Hidden Gems of the Loire Valley

While the iconic châteaux and vibrant towns of the Loire Valley draw plenty of visitors, the region also boasts some lesser-known treasures that are equally worth discovering. These hidden gems, from charming villages to unique historical sites, offer a quieter, more intimate experience of the Loire. Whether you're seeking peaceful countryside retreats, fascinating history, or natural beauty, these spots provide a delightful escape from the more crowded attractions.

Candes-Saint-Martin: A Picturesque Village on the Loire

Tucked away in the scenic Loire Valley, Candes-Saint-Martin is a village that feels like a step back in time. Sitting at the confluence of the Loire and Vienne rivers, this village is often overlooked by tourists, which makes it a perfect destination for those seeking peace and authenticity.

- Medieval Charm: Candes-Saint-Martin is a "Les Plus Beaux Villages de France" (One of France's Most Beautiful Villages) and offers a glimpse into traditional French village life. Its narrow, cobbled streets wind past white stone houses, and the Église Saint-Martin offers a peaceful place for reflection. The church, with its Gothic design, provides stunning views of the surrounding riverscape.

- Riverside Views: The village's location along the river makes it ideal for scenic strolls. Whether you choose to walk along the Loire or take a boat ride on the river, the peaceful atmosphere and the lush surroundings make this village a perfect spot for relaxation and quiet contemplation.

Montsoreau: A Village Steeped in History

Just a short distance from Candes-Saint-Martin, Montsoreau is another hidden gem, and it is known for its fascinating history and exceptional architecture. This charming village, perched on the banks of the Loire, is home to one of the most unique castles in the region, the Château de Montsoreau.

- Château de Montsoreau: What sets this château apart is its unique position—this Renaissance-era castle is built directly into the riverbanks of the Loire, giving it an unusual, almost ethereal appearance. Today, the château houses a museum of contemporary art, with rotating exhibitions that focus on the intersection of art, architecture, and history. The castle's peaceful gardens and its intimate setting make it a perfect spot for an afternoon visit.

- A Village Frozen in Time: The village itself retains much of its old-world charm, with winding lanes, timber-framed houses, and sweeping views of the Loire River. Walk through the village, enjoy the riverside views, and savor the quiet atmosphere that makes Montsoreau so unique.

Rochemenier: The Troglodyte Dwellings

For those interested in history and architecture, Rochemenier offers one of the Loire Valley's most fascinating hidden treasures. Located in the heart of the Anjou region, Rochemenier is famous for its troglodyte dwellings—homes carved directly into the rock of the cliffs.

- The Troglodyte Village: The Musée des Troglodytes is a must-visit for anyone curious about these subterranean homes. Rochemenier offers a glimpse into the lives of the people who once lived in these unique homes. The museum showcases troglodyte life, featuring a collection of preserved homes, tools, and artifacts that illustrate how these underground dwellings were used.

- Exploring the Caves: The troglodyte caves are cool and tranquil, even during the summer months, and they offer a fascinating insight into the region's history. These caves were used as homes, but also as storage spaces and shelters for livestock, making them a fascinating example of traditional rural life in the Loire.

Château de Montpoupon: A Lesser-Known Castle

While many visitors flock to the grand châteaux of the Loire, Château de Montpoupon offers a quieter, more intimate castle experience. Located in the heart of the Loir-et-Cher region, Montpoupon is a lesser-known gem, perfect for travelers seeking a quieter visit to the Loire's royal heritage.

- The Château: This beautiful 15th-century château is surrounded by lush greenery and tranquil gardens. Visitors can explore its well-preserved rooms, which showcase the history of the castle and its aristocratic residents. The château is renowned for its hunting exhibitions, which provide a deep dive into the region's historic connection to the art of hunting, and the La Chasse Museum, dedicated to the traditions of French hunting.

- Nature and Tranquility: Set within the rolling countryside of the Loire, Château de Montpoupon also offers beautiful nature walks. Wander through its gardens or explore the nearby forest paths for a peaceful, nature-filled experience that gives you a break from the more crowded destinations.

Forest Walks and Nature Escapes

Beyond the villages and castles, the Loire Valley is also a haven for nature lovers. The region offers an abundance of beautiful walking trails and natural parks, where you can experience the tranquility of the countryside.

- **Forêt de Chinon:** This expansive forest, located near the town of Chinon, offers an ideal escape into nature. With miles of walking and cycling trails, it's the perfect destination for hiking or simply enjoying the great outdoors. The forest is home to a variety of wildlife, and its paths lead you through dense woods, alongside streams, and into secluded glades.

- **The Loire à Vélo:** For those looking to combine nature with cycling, the Loire à Vélo is a fantastic cycling route that winds through vineyards, towns, and forests. The route takes you through some of the region's most beautiful landscapes, offering a different perspective on the Loire's natural beauty.

The Loire Valley is full of hidden gems waiting to be discovered. From the quiet charm of Candes-Saint-Martin to the fascinating troglodyte dwellings of Rochemenier, and the peaceful escape of Château de Montpoupon, these lesser-known spots provide a more intimate and unique experience of the region. Whether you're a history enthusiast, nature lover, or simply someone looking for tranquility away from the crowds, these hidden gems of the Loire will enrich your journey and leave you with lasting memories of this enchanting region.

CHAPTER 5: WHAT TO DO IN THE LOIRE VALLEY

The Loire Valley offers a wealth of activities that appeal to a range of interests, from outdoor adventures to cultural explorations. Whether you're an adrenaline seeker, a history enthusiast, or someone looking to enjoy the natural beauty of the region, the Loire Valley has something for everyone. Here's a closer look at some of the best things to do in this beautiful region.

Outdoor Adventures in the Loire Valley

The Loire Valley's stunning landscapes—rolling hills, vineyards, riverbanks, and forests—make it an ideal destination for outdoor activities. Whether you're interested in leisurely strolls, cycling, or exploring the natural beauty of the region, there's no shortage of adventures to enjoy.

Cycling along the Loire à Vélo Route

One of the most popular outdoor activities in the Loire Valley is cycling along the Loire à Vélo route, a dedicated cycling path that spans 800 kilometers from the city of Nevers to the Atlantic coast, following the meandering Loire River. The route takes cyclists through picturesque villages, expansive vineyards, historic towns, and some of the region's most iconic landmarks. It's a fantastic way to see the Loire Valley at a slower pace while enjoying its incredible natural beauty.

• The Scenic Route: Cycling the Loire à Vélo route offers a mix of scenic river views, charming countryside, and world-renowned vineyards. The route passes through famous destinations like Château de Chambord, Amboise, and Tours, as well as charming towns like Chaumont-sur-Loire and Chinon. Whether you're cycling a short section or the entire route, the journey is sure to be an unforgettable experience.

• Suitable for All Levels: The Loire à Vélo route is designed to be accessible to cyclists of all levels. The path is mostly flat and well-maintained, with easy-to-follow signs and plenty of places to stop for a break. You can also find rental stations along the route if you don't bring your own bike. For those who prefer a more relaxed pace, electric bikes are also available, making it easier to navigate some of the longer stretches.

• Cultural Stops Along the Way: As you cycle, you'll have the opportunity to stop and explore various cultural and historical attractions. Many of the towns along the Loire à Vélo route have local markets, museums, and, of course, world-famous châteaux. Take a detour to visit the Château de Villandry, with its meticulously landscaped gardens, or stop for a wine-tasting session in one of the valley's renowned vineyards. Cycling allows you to take in the region's diverse offerings, all while enjoying the beauty of the outdoors.

Hiking and Nature Walks

If cycling isn't your preferred activity, the Loire Valley offers numerous hiking trails and nature walks that allow you to immerse yourself in the region's tranquil landscapes. Whether you're exploring dense forests, walking along riverbanks, or trekking through vineyards, the Loire Valley is a great place to reconnect with nature.

• Forêt d'Amboise: For those who enjoy a walk through the woods, the Forêt d'Amboise is a peaceful forest near the town of Amboise. This forest is perfect for a relaxing walk, and there are several well-marked trails that lead through it. Along the way, you may spot wildlife and enjoy views of the Loire River in the distance.

• Loire Riverbanks: The Loire River itself is a major feature of the region's landscape, and walking along its banks is one of the most serene ways to experience the

Loire. Many towns, including Tours and Angers, have dedicated walking paths along the river that offer beautiful views of the water, nearby vineyards, and historic buildings.

• The Vineyards: The Loire Valley is known for its wine, and many of the vineyards offer walking tours where you can explore the countryside while learning about wine production. The Vouvray region, in particular, offers scenic walks through rolling hills covered in grapevines, giving you the chance to enjoy the countryside while also learning about the region's viticulture.

Water Sports and River Cruises

For those who prefer water-based activities, the Loire River offers a variety of options. Kayaking, canoeing, and even river cruises are popular ways to experience the region from a different perspective.

• Canoeing and Kayaking: If you want to be active on the water, canoeing or kayaking along the Loire River is a great option. There are several companies that offer rentals and guided tours, allowing you to explore the river's quiet stretches, pass under its charming bridges, and even paddle past the stunning châteaux that line the riverbanks.

• River Cruises: If you prefer a more leisurely pace, consider taking a river cruise on the Loire. Many boat tours are available, offering a relaxed way to see the valley's highlights while enjoying local food and wine. A river cruise lets you take in the beauty of the river and its surroundings while learning about the area's history and culture from knowledgeable guides.

Hot Air Ballooning

For a truly unique perspective on the Loire Valley, hot air ballooning offers an unforgettable way to experience the region's beauty from above. Several companies in the Loire Valley offer hot air balloon rides, providing a bird's-eye view of the valley's vineyards, châteaux, and rivers.

• Aerial Views: As the balloon floats gracefully above the Loire River and its rolling hills, you'll be treated to breathtaking panoramic views of the landscape below. The sight of the region's famous châteaux, such as Château de Chenonceau, from above is an experience you won't soon forget.

• Peaceful Adventure: Hot air ballooning is a tranquil, serene adventure that offers a peaceful way to take in the beauty of the Loire Valley. Whether you're celebrating a special occasion or simply looking for a unique experience, a hot air balloon ride offers an unforgettable way to explore the region.

Conclusion: Embrace the Outdoors in the Loire Valley

The Loire Valley's diverse landscape offers countless opportunities for outdoor adventures. From cycling along the Loire à Vélo route to hiking through scenic forests, there's no shortage of ways to experience the natural beauty of the region. Whether you're seeking a leisurely bike ride through the vineyards, a peaceful walk along the riverbanks, or an exhilarating hot air balloon ride, the Loire

Valley provides an ideal setting for outdoor exploration and adventure.

Wine & Gastronomy in the Loire Valley

The Loire Valley is not only known for its breathtaking châteaux and charming towns, but it's also a region steeped in a rich gastronomic tradition. The fertile soils and diverse climate make it one of France's most celebrated wine regions, and its culinary offerings are equally renowned. Whether you're a wine connoisseur, a casual enthusiast, or a foodie eager to savor the best of French cuisine, the Loire Valley promises an unforgettable experience.

Best Vineyards and Wine Tastings in the Loire Valley

The Loire Valley is home to a variety of wine regions, each offering its own distinct wines and exceptional tasting experiences. With a combination of centuries-old vineyards, family-run estates, and modern wineries, the Loire provides an incredible opportunity to explore French wine culture.

Sancerre: The Jewel of White Wine

Sancerre, located in the eastern Loire near the town of Bourges, is world-famous for its Sauvignon Blanc wines, which are among the most aromatic and vibrant white wines in France. The region is known for its steep vineyards, which are planted on the slopes of hills overlooking the Loire River. The chalky soil in Sancerre gives the wine its characteristic crispness, with notes of citrus, green apple, and fresh herbs.

- Wine Tastings: Many wineries in Sancerre offer guided tours of their vineyards, where you'll learn about the unique terroir that makes Sancerre wines so distinctive. Afterward, enjoy a tasting of the region's celebrated Sauvignon Blancs, along with local specialties such as goat cheese from the nearby villages. The Maison des Sancerre is an excellent place to start, offering both wine tastings and exhibitions on the region's wine history.

- Château de Sancerre: A visit to this historic château offers panoramic views over the vineyards and a chance to taste wines directly from the estate. Here, you can immerse yourself in the local wine culture, all while enjoying a view that perfectly complements the wines.

Vouvray: Sparkling Elegance

Situated in the central Loire Valley, Vouvray is known for its exquisite Chenin Blanc wines, which range from dry to sweet and even sparkling. The vineyards are located on the banks of the Loire River, and the cool climate of the region allows the grapes to develop a remarkable balance of acidity and sweetness.

- Wine Tastings: Vouvray's wine tastings are an essential experience. Many of the local estates, such as Domaine Huet and Domaine des Aubuisières, offer private tours where you can taste a variety of wines, including the region's signature sparkling Vouvray. These wines are known for their complexity, with flavors of stone fruits, honey, and hints of minerality. Many of these estates also produce organic wines, so it's worth checking out their sustainable practices.

• Vouvray Wine Festival: If you're visiting in the autumn, don't miss the annual Fête des Vins de Vouvray, which celebrates the harvest season with a vibrant wine festival featuring tastings, live music, and local food.

Chinon: The Heart of Red Wine

Chinon, located in the western Loire Valley, is one of the region's most famous wine-producing areas, particularly for its Cabernet Franc wines. The vineyards are set in a stunning landscape of rolling hills and medieval castles, with the iconic Château de Chinon overlooking the town. The wines here are known for their deep, dark fruit flavors and smoky, earthy undertones.

• Wine Tastings: Chinon's wine-tasting experiences are a must for any wine lover. The Domaine Bernard Baudry is one of the region's most celebrated estates, known for producing elegant, full-bodied reds. At Domaine de la Noblaie, you can taste wines directly from the vineyards while learning about the ancient winemaking techniques that make Chinon wines so distinctive.

• Château de Chinon: In addition to being a historical site, the Château de Chinon also offers wine-tasting tours where you can sip on local wines while exploring the castle's fascinating history. The views over the vineyards and the Loire River from the château are spectacular, adding to the allure of the wine-tasting experience.

Loire Valley Gastronomy: Savoring the Region's Flavors

In addition to its wines, the Loire Valley boasts a rich culinary tradition, from delicious cheeses and charcuterie to fresh seafood and hearty meats. The region's gastronomy is heavily influenced by its agricultural abundance, with local products like goat cheese, rillettes, and fresh fish from the Loire River playing a central role in its cuisine.

Cheese: A Loire Specialty

The Loire Valley is home to some of France's best-loved cheeses. A must-try is Crottin de Chavignol, a small, tangy goat cheese from the Sancerre region. Other regional cheeses include Saint-Maure de Touraine, a soft goat cheese with a smoky flavor, and Valençay, a pyramid-shaped cheese made from cow's milk.

- Cheese and Wine Pairing: Many vineyards in the Loire Valley offer cheese pairings with their wines. A classic pairing is the fresh Crottin de Chavignol with a crisp Sancerre. In Vouvray, try a rich Chenin Blanc with a creamy Saint-Maure de Touraine for an unforgettable taste experience.

Local Specialties

In addition to wine and cheese, there are several culinary delights you should not miss while in the Loire Valley:

- Rillettes: This rich, spreadable pork pâté is a Loire Valley specialty. It's often served on a baguette with pickles or enjoyed as part of a charcuterie board.

- Tarte Tatin: A delicious upside-down caramelized apple tart that originated in the Loire Valley. It's perfect for dessert after a day of wine tasting.

- Fougasse: A type of flatbread flavored with olive oil and herbs, often served as an appetizer.

A Complete Loire Experience: Wine, Food, and Culture

No trip to the Loire Valley is complete without exploring the local food and wine scene. Whether you're tasting a delicate Vouvray wine, savoring a rich rillettes with a glass of Chinon, or enjoying a classic tarte Tatin, the Loire Valley offers a culinary journey that perfectly complements its natural beauty and rich history. Make sure to spend time in the vineyards, sit down for a leisurely meal in one of the charming local restaurants, and enjoy the flavors of the region—it's all part of the experience.

Regional Specialties in the Loire Valley

The Loire Valley is a gastronomic paradise, with its rich agricultural landscape offering a delightful array of regional specialties. From classic French desserts to tangy cheeses and hearty charcuterie, the Loire's culinary traditions reflect both its natural abundance and its cultural history.

Tarte Tatin: The Iconic Upside-Down Tart

One of the Loire Valley's most famous regional desserts is Tarte Tatin, an upside-down apple tart that's beloved across France and beyond. Legend has it that the dessert was created by accident at the Hôtel Tatin in Lamotte-Beuvron when the Tatin sisters mistakenly overcooked the apples for a traditional apple pie. Rather than tossing them out, they placed a pastry crust on top and baked the mixture to perfection, creating the now-famous caramelized treat.

- Taste: The tart features sweet, caramelized apples with a rich, buttery flavor, all encased in a flaky pastry. It's often served warm with a dollop of whipped cream or a scoop of vanilla ice cream.

- Where to Find It: Tarte Tatin is commonly served in most local bakeries and restaurants across the Loire Valley. You can find a particularly delicious version at La Tarte Tatin in Lamotte-Beuvron, the birthplace of the tart. Alternatively, look for it in many Loire-region restaurants that embrace traditional French cooking.

Crottin de Chavignol: A Taste of Goat Cheese Tradition

The Crottin de Chavignol is a small, creamy goat cheese with a distinct tang, produced in the Sancerre region of the Loire. This cheese has been made for centuries, and its name comes from the word "crottin," which refers to a small, traditional clay pot used for storing the cheese. Crottin de Chavignol is often enjoyed both young and aged, with the older versions becoming firmer and more flavorful.

- Taste: The cheese is creamy and slightly tangy when young, and more intense and earthy when aged. It pairs perfectly with a glass of Sancerre wine, the crisp Sauvignon Blanc that the region is famous for.

- Where to Find It: Crottin de Chavignol is widely available at local markets, cheese shops, and vineyards throughout the Loire Valley. In Sancerre, the Maison des Sancerre offers an excellent introduction to the cheese, often pairing it with wine tastings.

Suggested Local Markets and Eateries

The Loire Valley's culinary treasures can be discovered in its bustling local markets, where fresh produce, artisanal products, and regional specialties abound. These markets are not only great for shopping but also offer the chance to sample local delicacies, meet passionate producers, and immerse yourself in the flavors of the region.

Local Markets to Explore

- Tours Market (Les Halles de Tours): Located in the heart of the historic city of Tours, this vibrant market is a must-visit for food lovers. With over 100 stalls, it offers an impressive variety of fresh fruits, vegetables, meats, cheeses, and fish. Don't miss the chance to pick up some Crottin de Chavignol or local wines while exploring the market. The covered market is open every day, except Monday, and offers an authentic taste of the Loire.

- **Chinon Market:** Situated in the medieval town of Chinon, this market offers a beautiful mix of local products, including artisanal cheeses, meats, and fresh produce. You'll find many local specialties such as rillettes (pâté), fresh Loire fish, and a variety of fruits and vegetables. The market is open on Saturdays, making it an ideal stop for a weekend visit.

• **Amboise Market:** Held every Sunday morning, the market in Amboise is known for its regional produce, gourmet treats, and handicrafts. It's a great place to sample the Loire's famous goat cheeses and stock up on fresh ingredients for a picnic by the Loire River.

Suggested Eateries

For a more in-depth taste of the Loire Valley's cuisine, enjoy a meal at one of the region's many charming eateries. From casual bistros to Michelin-starred restaurants, the Loire offers a range of dining experiences that showcase its culinary traditions.

• **Le Bistrot des Halles (Tours):** Located near the market in Tours, this cozy bistro is the perfect spot for a traditional Loire meal. The menu focuses on local specialties, including rillettes and pâté en croûte, and the wine list is extensive, featuring wines from across the Loire Valley. It's an excellent place to enjoy a warm, hearty meal after browsing the market.

• **Les Hautes Roches (Rochecorbon):** Set in a cliffside overlooking the Loire River, this Michelin-starred restaurant offers a refined dining experience with spectacular views. The menu features seasonal ingredients from the Loire Valley, including local fish, meats, and cheeses, with perfectly paired Loire wines. It's an elegant spot to indulge in a more upscale version of the region's culinary delights.

- **Auberge de la Musardière (Montargis):** A charming rural inn where you can taste authentic Tarte Tatin and other traditional Loire desserts. The cozy atmosphere and friendly service make this a wonderful spot for a leisurely lunch or dinner after a day of exploring the countryside.

- **Le Cheval Blanc (Chinon):** Situated in the heart of Chinon, this classic French restaurant serves up both classic and contemporary French dishes. The menu often features regional specialties such as goat cheese salads, rillettes, and braised lamb with a glass of local red wine.

Pairing Loire Wines with Local Cuisine

No meal in the Loire Valley is complete without a glass of the region's outstanding wine. The Loire is known for a wide range of wines, from the crisp Sauvignon Blanc of Sancerre to the rich, full-bodied reds of Chinon. Here are a few classic pairings to enjoy with the region's specialties:

- **Sancerre Wine with Crottin de Chavignol:** The acidity and minerality of Sancerre's Sauvignon Blanc complements the tangy, creamy texture of Crottin de Chavignol, creating a perfect match for a light, refreshing pairing.

- **Chinon Red Wine with Rillettes:** The deep, fruity flavors of Cabernet Franc from the Chinon region pair beautifully with the rich, savory flavors of rillettes. The wine's structure balances the fattiness of the pâté, making this pairing a Loire classic.

- **Vouvray with Tarte Tatin**: A glass of sparkling Vouvray complements the sweet, caramelized flavors of the Tarte Tatin, offering a bright contrast to the dessert's richness.

By visiting these local markets and dining at these charming eateries, you can immerse yourself in the true flavors of the Loire Valley, experiencing the region's culinary heritage in the most authentic way. Whether you're savoring a slice of Tarte Tatin or enjoying a glass of Sancerre with a plate of goat cheese, the Loire Valley offers an unforgettable gastronomic journey.

Cultural Highlights of the Loire Valley

The Loire Valley is not only renowned for its picturesque landscapes, fairytale châteaux, and world-class wines but also for its vibrant cultural scene. The region offers an array of events and festivals that celebrate its rich heritage, artistic traditions, and historical significance. Whether you're interested in music, arts, or traditional celebrations, the Loire's cultural highlights provide a chance to dive deeper into the heart of French culture.

Loire Music and Arts Festivals

Throughout the year, the Loire Valley hosts a variety of music and arts festivals that showcase the region's artistic heritage and contemporary creativity. These festivals are an essential part of the Loire's cultural fabric, bringing together artists, musicians, and visitors from around the world.

- **Festival de Loire (Orléans):** Held every two years, this popular festival in the city of Orléans is a celebration of the Loire River and its maritime heritage. The festival features live music, boat parades, historical reenactments, and street performances. It's a vibrant event that highlights the river's central role in shaping the culture of the region. From folk music to jazz performances, there's something for everyone, with many events taking place along the banks of the Loire River.

- **Festival d'Anjou (Angers):** This renowned arts festival takes place in the city of Angers each summer and is dedicated to theater and performing arts. Staging both contemporary and classical plays, the festival is held at various venues, including the stunning Château d'Angers, where you can enjoy performances against the backdrop of the castle's medieval walls. It's an opportunity to immerse yourself in French theatrical traditions while enjoying the region's historic settings.

- **La Route des Vins en Musique (Vineyards of the Loire):** This unique music festival combines the best of the Loire Valley's wine country with live performances. Held in the summer months, the festival features classical and contemporary music concerts set in the vineyards, often with wine tastings and food pairings. The backdrop of the vineyards adds a magical element to the experience, making it an unforgettable way to combine art, music, and gastronomy.

- **Le Printemps des Comédiens (Montargis):** A celebration of modern theater, this festival is held each spring in Montargis and features a series of performances that explore a range of artistic expressions, from drama to dance. The performances are staged in both traditional theaters and open-air venues, allowing you to experience the art in a variety of settings.

Historical Events and Traditional Celebrations

The Loire Valley is steeped in history, and its grand châteaux provide the perfect setting for historical reenactments and traditional celebrations that bring the past to life. These events offer a unique opportunity to step back in time and experience the medieval and Renaissance eras as they were lived by royalty, nobility, and common folk.

- **Jousting Displays at Château de Chinon:** The Château de Chinon, a medieval fortress that once housed kings, is the site of regular jousting displays and medieval festivals. These exciting events recreate the chivalric traditions of the past, with knights in full armor competing in thrilling jousts and archery contests. The jousting tournaments are often held during summer festivals, allowing visitors to witness firsthand the grandeur and spectacle of the medieval world. It's a fun and interactive way to experience the Loire's rich history.

- **Medieval Festival at Château de Loches:** In Loches, another of the Loire Valley's stunning châteaux, you can experience the annual Medieval Festival, where the castle grounds are transformed into a vibrant medieval marketplace. The event features costumed performers, medieval music, traditional crafts, and jousting. The historical atmosphere of the château adds authenticity to the festivities, offering visitors a glimpse into the past through the sights and sounds of the Middle Ages.

- Renaissance Celebrations at Château de Chambord: The grand Château de Chambord, one of the most iconic Renaissance châteaux in the Loire, hosts annual events celebrating the grandeur of the French Renaissance. Visitors can enjoy reenactments of Renaissance court life, featuring musicians, dancers, and actors in period costumes. The château's spectacular architecture and lush grounds provide a breathtaking backdrop for these lively events, which celebrate the arts, music, and royal traditions of the 16th century.

- **Fête de la Saint-Martin (Tours):** In Tours, the Fête de la Saint-Martin is a lively annual event celebrating the patron saint of the city. The festival includes processions, music, and traditional dances. The streets come alive with colorful parades and performances that reflect the region's deep-rooted cultural traditions. It's a wonderful way to immerse yourself in the local customs and festive atmosphere of the Loire Valley.

Experiencing Loire's Cultural Essence

Whether you're attending a world-class music festival, experiencing medieval jousting, or celebrating traditional French holidays, the Loire Valley's cultural highlights offer something for every traveler. These events allow you to engage with the region's rich heritage and artistic spirit in a way that's deeply personal and immersive. Whether you're a lover of music, history, or tradition, the Loire's cultural calendar is a perfect complement to its natural beauty and iconic landmarks. Embrace the rhythm of the Loire Valley, where art, history, and tradition come together in spectacular fashion.

These cultural events, festivals, and reenactments are not just about observing the past—they invite you to step into history and experience it firsthand. From the medieval jousts to the modern arts, the Loire Valley offers a rich tapestry of cultural experiences that will leave you with lasting memories.

CHAPTER 6: PRACTICAL INFORMATION FOR THE LOIRE VALLEY

The Loire Valley, with its picturesque villages, vast vineyards, and fairytale châteaux, is a region best explored at your own pace. Whether you're venturing through charming towns, cycling along scenic routes, or visiting iconic landmarks, understanding how to navigate the region will enhance your experience. Here's everything you need to know about transportation and getting around the Loire Valley, including tips on parking and navigating by car, train, or bike.

Navigating the Loire Valley by Car

The Loire Valley is well connected by a network of highways and smaller roads, making it an ideal region to explore by car. Renting a car gives you the flexibility to discover the charming villages, hidden gems, and vineyards at your own pace, especially if you plan to visit more remote areas.

• **Rental Cars:** Major car rental companies are available in nearby cities like Tours, Orléans, and Angers, as well as at the Tours Val de Loire Airport. Most rental agencies offer convenient pick-up and drop-off locations. Keep in mind that renting a car is ideal for exploring the countryside and accessing the region's more remote attractions, such as small villages and lesser-known châteaux.

• **Driving in the Loire:** Roads are generally in excellent condition, and the speed limits vary: 130 km/h (81 mph) on highways, 90 km/h (56 mph) on main roads, and 50 km/h (31 mph) in towns. Be mindful of local traffic signs, especially in smaller towns where roads can be narrow. Many of the rural roads are scenic, so take time to enjoy the views while driving.

• **Toll Roads:** Some highways in the Loire Valley are toll roads (péage). These are typically well-maintained and allow for quicker travel between major towns like Tours, Orléans, and Angers. You can pay tolls in cash or with a credit card at automated kiosks along the highway.

• **Car Parking Tips:** When visiting popular sites like Château de Chambord or Château de Chenonceau, parking is usually available near the entrance. However, during peak seasons, these parking lots can fill up quickly. It's recommended to arrive early in the day to secure a spot. In towns like Tours or Orléans, be prepared for limited street parking in the city center. Look for designated parking areas or use public parking garages.

Navigating by Train

The Loire Valley is well-served by France's high-speed rail network (TGV), as well as regional trains that connect the region's major cities and towns. Traveling by train is a convenient, eco-friendly, and relaxing way to see the Loire Valley.

• **TGV High-Speed Trains:** The TGV trains provide fast and efficient connections from Paris to key cities in the Loire Valley, such as Tours, Orléans, and Angers. Travel times from Paris to Tours, for example, are around 1.5 to 2 hours, making it a great option for day trips. For tickets, you can book in advance through the official SNCF website or use a rail pass if you're traveling extensively by train in France.

• **Regional Trains:** The TER (Transport Express Régional) trains are slower but offer more affordable options to reach smaller towns and rural areas. These regional trains connect cities like Tours, Blois, and Saumur, and often provide access to more scenic routes. If you're planning to explore villages or vineyards not directly accessible by the TGV, TER trains are a good choice.

• **Train Stations:** Major train stations in the Loire Valley, such as Gare de Tours and Gare d'Orléans, are centrally located and well-equipped with amenities like waiting areas, cafes, and shops. When arriving at smaller towns or villages, train stations are often close to the city center, making it easy to continue your exploration.

• **Tickets and Passes:** You can purchase tickets online in advance or at train stations. Consider purchasing a France Rail Pass if you plan on taking multiple train journeys, as it can save you money on fares.

Cycling in the Loire Valley

The Loire Valley is a cyclist's paradise, offering miles of bike-friendly paths and scenic routes that pass through vineyards, forests, and along the banks of the Loire River. Whether you're an experienced cyclist or a casual rider, biking is one of the best ways to immerse yourself in the region's beauty.

• **Loire à Vélo:** This well-marked, 800-kilometer (500-mile) cycling route stretches from Cuffy near Nevers to Saint-Nazaire on the Atlantic coast, passing through many of the Loire Valley's iconic châteaux and charming towns. The route is divided into manageable sections, making it suitable for both beginner and experienced cyclists. Along the way, you'll enjoy spectacular views of the Loire River and vineyards, as well as stops at sites like Château de Chambord, Château de Chenonceau, and Tours.

• **Renting a Bike:** Bicycles can be rented from various shops in towns like Tours, Angers, or Blois, or even at designated stations along the Loire à Vélo route. Many bike rental companies offer electric bikes for a more relaxed ride, especially if you want to explore the countryside with ease. Some companies also provide guided tours for those who prefer a structured cycling experience.

• **Cycling Tips:** The Loire Valley is generally flat, but some areas—particularly around the châteaux—can be hilly. Always bring water, sunscreen, and a map or GPS device. If you're riding along the Loire à Vélo route, there are plenty of places to stop for rest, food, and sightseeing.

Parking Near Popular Sites

When visiting popular châteaux and tourist spots, parking is generally available but can fill up quickly, especially during peak tourist seasons. Here are a few tips for parking:

• **Château Parking:** Most major châteaux such as Château de Chambord, Château de Chenonceau, and Château d'Angers have large parking lots, which are usually free or require a small fee. These lots are typically within walking distance of the entrance.

• **Small Villages and Towns:** In small towns like Montargis or Saumur, parking is often limited in the town center. Look for public parking areas or use underground or multi-story parking garages if available.

• **Street Parking:** In cities like Tours or Orléans, pay attention to parking signs and meters. You may need to use coins or cards for street parking, and parking regulations are strictly enforced, so be sure to check the hours and avoid fines.

Navigating the Loire Valley is straightforward with a car, train, or bike, depending on your preferences. Each mode of transportation offers its own advantages—whether it's the freedom of the open road, the convenience of high-speed trains, or the beauty of cycling through the vineyards. With a little planning and preparation, you'll be able to explore the Loire Valley's many treasures with ease.

Accommodation Options in the Loire Valley

Whether you're looking for a luxurious stay fit for royalty, a charming bed and breakfast nestled in the countryside, or something more unusual, the Loire Valley offers a wide range of accommodation to suit every taste and budget. From grand château hotels to quaint boutique stays and unique lodgings, here's an overview of the best places to rest during your journey through this stunning region.

Best Château Stays for a Luxurious Experience

For a truly unforgettable experience, why not spend a night in one of the Loire Valley's iconic châteaux? These fairy-tale castles often offer luxurious accommodations, combining history, opulence, and exceptional service. Waking up in a grand suite, surrounded by centuries of history, is a dream come true for many visitors.

- **Château de Chambord:** This Renaissance masterpiece is not just a must-see for its architecture and grounds, but also offers exclusive stays in its beautifully restored rooms. The château itself is a UNESCO World Heritage site, and some rooms overlook its vast estate and the Loire River. Staying here means stepping into the life of French nobility.

- **Château de Chenonceau:** Known as the "Château of the Ladies" due to its fascinating history with powerful women, this castle offers a luxurious and historic stay. Enjoy accommodations in beautifully furnished rooms, many of which provide scenic views of the château's gardens and the river. Dining options also showcase local cuisine, making it an ideal choice for a romantic getaway.

- **Château de Noizay:** Located in the heart of the Loire Valley wine region, Château de Noizay offers elegant rooms, a tranquil atmosphere, and access to wine-tasting experiences in the château's own vineyards. It's perfect for wine lovers looking to combine luxury with the charm of a historic château.

These châteaux often come with gourmet restaurants, spa services, and well-manicured grounds perfect for leisurely walks. If you want to experience the Loire Valley in true luxury, a stay in one of these châteaux will provide an unforgettable and royal experience.

Budget-Friendly B&Bs and Boutique Hotels

While the Loire Valley offers many luxurious accommodations, it's also home to a wide variety of charming and budget-friendly bed and breakfasts (B&Bs) and boutique hotels. These options provide comfort, character, and local flavor, often at a fraction of the cost of château stays.

- **La Maison Jules (Tours):** Situated in the heart of Tours, this boutique B&B offers contemporary design mixed with a welcoming atmosphere. It's an excellent base for exploring the city and nearby vineyards. The owners are happy to recommend local eateries, and the rooms are designed to ensure a relaxing stay at affordable rates.

- **Le Clos de L'Hermitage (Amboise):** Nestled in the town of Amboise, this quaint B&B provides a cozy and intimate atmosphere. Guests can enjoy beautifully appointed rooms, a peaceful garden, and a delicious breakfast with homemade jams. Its proximity to Château d'Amboise makes it an ideal choice for visitors looking to explore the town and surrounding area.

- **Hotel Le Choiseul (Chenonceaux):** While a little pricier than some, this boutique hotel offers great value, with rooms overlooking the picturesque village of Chenonceaux and just a short walk from the famous château. It combines contemporary comforts with a historic setting, and its restaurant serves fresh, locally sourced cuisine.

- **Le Relais de la Haute Ville (Saumur):** Located in the charming town of Saumur, this small, budget-friendly boutique hotel offers clean, well-equipped rooms with a homey feel. Guests can easily walk to Saumur's Château de Saumur, making it a convenient and affordable base for exploring the region.

These affordable yet charming B&Bs and boutique hotels offer great value for money, perfect for travelers who want to experience the Loire without breaking the bank. Many of these establishments also provide excellent local tips for exploring the area, ensuring that your stay is both comfortable and enriching.

Unique Stays: Troglodyte Lodgings and More

For those seeking something truly unusual, the Loire Valley offers a variety of unique and one-of-a-kind accommodations. If you're looking for an authentic, immersive experience, consider staying in a troglodyte dwelling—ancient cave homes that have been carved into the region's soft limestone cliffs.

- **Les Troglodytes de la Cave (Rochemenier):** This charming site offers visitors the chance to stay in traditional troglodyte dwellings that have been restored for comfort while preserving their rustic charm. The rooms are cool in the summer and cozy in the winter, making it a great option for a unique, off-the-beaten-path stay.

- **La Cave de Pommeau (Saumur):** Nestled in the heart of Saumur's vineyards, this accommodation offers the experience of staying in a converted wine cave. The cave's thick walls keep the rooms cool in the summer and provide a unique atmosphere, with the added bonus of being surrounded by vineyards. It's perfect for wine lovers looking for something distinct.

- **Domaine de la Pléneuf (Chinon):** This eco-friendly, troglodyte-style accommodation combines sustainable design with ancient cave living. The rooms are set within the cliffside, offering a calm and serene retreat. It's an excellent choice for travelers looking to experience the Loire's natural beauty in a unique way.

Aside from troglodyte lodgings, there are other unique options in the Loire Valley, including converted barns, boutique farmhouses, and riverboats along the Loire River. These distinctive accommodations offer a more personal, intimate experience and a chance to truly immerse yourself in the region's culture.

Conclusion

The Loire Valley offers a wide range of accommodation options to suit every traveler, from luxurious château stays to budget-friendly B&Bs and unique troglodyte dwellings. Whether you're seeking opulence or a quirky, offbeat experience, the region's diverse accommodations will provide you with a comfortable and memorable base for your adventures.

Budgeting for Your Trip to the Loire Valley

Traveling through the Loire Valley doesn't have to break the bank. With a bit of planning, you can experience the region's beauty, history, and culture on a budget. Here are some tips for keeping your trip affordable, along with suggestions for inexpensive dining and activities, as well as free or low-cost attractions.

Affordable Dining in the Loire Valley

The Loire Valley is renowned for its rich culinary heritage, but that doesn't mean you have to spend a fortune to enjoy its delicious cuisine. Here are a few tips for eating affordably without sacrificing quality:

• Local Markets: One of the best ways to enjoy fresh, local produce and authentic flavors at a low cost is by visiting the region's bustling farmers' markets. Cities like Tours, Saumur, and Amboise host vibrant markets, where you can pick up fresh bread, cheese, charcuterie, and fruits. These ingredients can easily form the basis of a simple, picnic-style meal that will allow you to enjoy the Loire's picturesque surroundings without the need to splurge on a sit-down restaurant.

• Bakeries and Bistros: For a quick, inexpensive meal, look out for local bakeries offering sandwiches, croissants, or quiches. These are perfect for a light lunch on the go. Many small bistros also offer daily plat du jour (dish of the day), which is often an affordable and filling option, typically ranging from €12 to €20 for a complete meal.

• Wine Tastings: While wine tasting at a château can be pricey, there are smaller, family-run vineyards throughout the Loire Valley that offer more affordable tastings, often with the option to buy bottles directly from the vineyard at lower prices. Visiting these smaller wineries can be a great way to sample the region's famous wines without the high cost of luxury wine tours.

• Street Food and Food Trucks: In larger cities like Tours, you'll often find food trucks or street vendors selling local snacks, such as crepes or French sausages, which can be both filling and affordable. These options provide a taste of local flavor without the price tag of a full restaurant meal.

Inexpensive Activities and Attractions

While the Loire Valley is known for its magnificent châteaux, many of them can be quite costly to visit. However, there are plenty of affordable or even free activities to enjoy throughout the region. Here are a few ideas:

• Free Visits to Towns and Villages: The charming towns and villages of the Loire Valley, such as Candes-Saint-Martin, Montsoreau, and Chinon, offer a great way to explore the region's beauty at no cost. Walking around the medieval streets, visiting local markets, and admiring the architecture of the town squares are all free activities that allow you to experience the culture and history of the area.

• Cycling Along the Loire à Vélo Route: One of the best ways to explore the Loire Valley on a budget is by cycling along the Loire à Vélo route. This 800-km trail follows the Loire River, passing vineyards, quaint villages, and historical landmarks. Renting a bike is often inexpensive, and the trail itself is free to access. Whether you choose to cycle the entire route or just a portion, it's a great way to enjoy the region's natural beauty and connect with its culture on a budget.

• Château Gardens and Grounds: Many of the region's châteaux offer free access to their gardens and surrounding grounds, even if entry to the château itself requires a ticket. For example, you can explore the Château de Chaumont-sur-Loire's stunning gardens without paying for the full château entry fee. These expansive grounds often offer magnificent views of the Loire River and are perfect for a peaceful afternoon stroll.

• Visit Local Vineyards: While wine tastings can be pricey, many of the Loire Valley's vineyards allow free or low-cost visits to their vineyards and cellars, especially smaller family-run estates. You can enjoy walking through the vineyards and learning about the wine-making process without spending much money.

• Cultural Events and Festivals: The Loire Valley hosts numerous free or low-cost festivals throughout the year, including music festivals, outdoor theater performances, and local celebrations. Many towns, especially Tours and Saumur, have vibrant arts scenes, where you can catch free or affordable performances in local parks or public spaces. Check local event calendars for opportunities to enjoy the region's cultural offerings at a fraction of the cost.

More Free or Low-Cost Attractions

• Loire River Cruises: While private boat tours can be expensive, some smaller towns offer boat rentals or small group cruises along the Loire River at more affordable prices. Alternatively, you can enjoy the riverbanks and scenic views for free, perfect for a relaxing afternoon.

• Hiking Trails: The Loire Valley boasts several beautiful hiking trails that are free to use. For example, the Parc Naturel Régional Loire-Anjou-Touraine offers numerous trails through protected landscapes, forests, and vineyards. These trails are a fantastic way to enjoy the region's natural beauty without spending a dime.

- Museums with Free Admission: Some smaller museums in the Loire Valley offer free admission or discounted rates for students, seniors, or children. Musée des Beaux-Arts in Tours and the Musée d'Histoire Naturelle in Angers are examples of museums with affordable or no-cost entry on certain days of the week.

The Loire Valley is not just a destination for those with deep pockets—it offers numerous affordable experiences that allow travelers to enjoy its beauty and charm on a budget. By exploring the local markets, enjoying free attractions, cycling through the vineyards, and taking advantage of low-cost dining options, you can experience the region's best offerings without overspending. With a little planning and a focus on local experiences, the Loire Valley can be an affordable yet unforgettable adventure.

CHAPTER 7: SAMPLE ITINERARIES FOR THE LOIRE VALLEY

The Loire Valley offers a rich variety of experiences, from its fairytale châteaux and picturesque vineyards to charming towns and natural beauty. Whether you have three days or a full week, this region is perfect for exploring at a leisurely pace. Below, we've outlined two sample itineraries designed to give you a well-rounded taste of the Loire Valley.

3-Day Highlights Tour: Iconic Châteaux and Wine Tastings

If you're short on time but want to see the best the Loire Valley has to offer, this 3-day itinerary focuses on the most iconic châteaux, picturesque villages, and wine tastings.

Day 1: Discover the Majestic Châteaux

- Morning: Château de Chambord

Start your trip by visiting Château de Chambord, the largest and most famous château in the Loire Valley. Known for its distinctive Renaissance architecture and expansive grounds, Chambord is a must-see. Arrive early to avoid crowds and enjoy a leisurely walk through the estate's grounds or even a boat ride along the river that flows through it.

- Lunch: Local Bistro

After exploring Chambord, head to a nearby village for a traditional French lunch at a local bistro. Enjoy regional specialties such as crotin de Chavignol (a local goat cheese) paired with a glass of Loire wine.

- Afternoon: Château de Cheverny

In the afternoon, visit Château de Cheverny, a more intimate but equally charming château with its perfectly manicured gardens and detailed interiors. If you're a fan of the Tintin comic books, you'll notice the château's resemblance to the one featured in the series.

- Evening: Wine Tasting in the Vouvray Region

Finish your day with a wine tasting in Vouvray, a region known for its white wines made from Chenin Blanc grapes. Visit a local vineyard for a guided tour and tasting session, enjoying the breathtaking views over the vineyards as the sun sets.

Day 2: Exploring Tours and the Heart of the Loire

- Morning: Tours

Begin your second day in the city of Tours, the capital of the Indre-et-Loire department. Wander the charming old town, with its cobblestone streets, medieval buildings, and bustling Place Plumereau. If you're a fan of history, visit the Musée des Beaux-Arts to explore its extensive collection of art.

- Lunch: Tours Local Market

Stop for lunch at the Les Halles de Tours, a local market where you can sample a variety of regional products. Enjoy a selection of fresh cheeses, meats, and pastries, and make sure to try Tarte Tatin, a local dessert.

- Afternoon: Château de Villandry

After lunch, head to Château de Villandry, famous for its stunning Renaissance gardens. Take your time strolling through the gardens, which are considered some of the most beautiful in France. The château itself is worth exploring, with its beautiful rooms and panoramic views over the gardens.

- Evening: Dinner in Amboise

Finish your day with a short drive to Amboise, a picturesque town on the banks of the Loire River. Enjoy dinner at a local restaurant overlooking the river, where you can sample more Loire Valley specialties like duck confit or rillettes.

Day 3: Wine and Villages of the Loire

- Morning: Chinon and Wine Tasting

On your final day, head to the charming town of Chinon, known for its medieval château and red wine. Explore the cobbled streets, visit the Château de Chinon, and enjoy panoramic views of the surrounding vineyards. Stop for a wine tasting at one of the local wineries, known for their exceptional red wines.

- Lunch: Scenic Picnic in the Vineyards

Grab some local cheeses, bread, and wine, and head into the countryside for a peaceful picnic surrounded by vineyards. Many vineyards offer picnic areas with stunning views where you can relax and enjoy the scenery.

- Afternoon: Explore Villages like Montsoreau

After your picnic, spend the afternoon exploring Montsoreau, a beautiful village located along the Loire River. The village is home to Château de Montsoreau, which is now a contemporary art museum. Wander the narrow streets, admire the charming architecture, and perhaps enjoy a coffee at a café by the river.

- Evening: Sunset Views Over the Loire

End your trip with a final stop at the Château de Langeais, a less touristy but equally captivating château. Explore its impressive medieval structure and enjoy the sunset from the château's towers, overlooking the Loire Valley.

Ideal for:

- Wine lovers eager to taste some of France's finest wines, especially those made in the Loire Valley.

- History enthusiasts wanting to explore France's most famous châteaux and medieval villages.

- Those looking for a balanced itinerary that combines cultural highlights, nature, and local gastronomy.

This 3-day itinerary covers the best of the Loire Valley, from its majestic châteaux to its renowned vineyards, ensuring that you experience the region's beauty, culture, and culinary delights at a relaxed and manageable pace.

5-Day Immersion: A Mix of Famous Spots and Lesser-Known Gems

If you have five days to explore the Loire Valley, this immersive itinerary offers a balanced mix of iconic châteaux, picturesque villages, outdoor adventures, and cultural experiences. This is perfect for those who want to dig deeper into the region's charm, from historical landmarks to hidden gems that will give you a true taste of the Loire's unique appeal. Whether you're a solo traveler, a couple, or a family, this itinerary offers something for everyone.

Day 1: Introduction to the Loire Valley's Icons

- Morning: Château de Chambord

Start your immersion into the Loire Valley with the grand Château de Chambord, arguably the most iconic château in the region. Known for its distinctive French Renaissance style and sweeping grounds, Chambord offers a perfect first stop. Explore the château's extravagant interiors, and take a walk through the surrounding forest or even rent a bike to explore the estate's vast grounds.

- Lunch: Lunch in Blois

After visiting Chambord, head to the nearby town of Blois for a delicious lunch. Blois is home to charming cafes and bistros where you can try regional dishes such as rillettes (a meat spread) and Tarte Tatin.

- Afternoon: Château de Cheverny

A short drive from Blois, visit Château de Cheverny. This château is famed for its beautiful gardens, detailed interior, and as the inspiration for the Tintin comic book series. Don't miss the stunning Hound Pack that roams the estate.

- Evening: Dinner in Tours

Spend your first evening in Tours, a central city known for its lively atmosphere. Wander the old town and enjoy dinner at one of the many restaurants offering Loire specialties such as duck confit or Chinon wine.

Day 2: Vineyards and Historical Exploration

- Morning: Wine Tasting in Sancerre

Dedicate the morning to one of the Loire Valley's best-known wine regions: Sancerre. Famous for its white wines made from Sauvignon Blanc, Sancerre is ideal for a guided vineyard tour and wine tasting. Explore the picturesque vineyards and enjoy tasting some of the world's finest wines while learning about the history of the region's wine production.

- Lunch: Picnic in the Vineyards

Pack a picnic with fresh local ingredients, or visit a local market to buy goodies for a lunch in the countryside. Enjoy a peaceful break among the rows of grapevines with sweeping views of the Loire Valley.

- Afternoon: Château de Villandry Gardens

After lunch, head to Château de Villandry, known for its beautifully designed Renaissance gardens. Wander through the intricate geometric flowerbeds, vegetable gardens, and water features. The château's garden is perfect for those seeking tranquility and beauty.

- Evening: Explore Amboise

Finish the day in the town of Amboise, where you can explore the quaint streets and enjoy dinner at a local restaurant. If you have time, take a brief visit to the

Château d'Amboise, which offers impressive views of the Loire River.

Day 3: A Family-Friendly Day in Nature and History

- Morning: Visit Château de Chenonceau

Start your day at Château de Chenonceau, one of the Loire Valley's most beloved châteaux. This family-friendly château has a rich history and is surrounded by beautiful gardens, perfect for kids to explore. The château spans the River Cher and has an incredible collection of art and furniture.

- Lunch: Local Bistro in Chenonceaux

After touring the château, stop for lunch in the village of Chenonceaux. Enjoy traditional French cuisine, such as coq au vin or fresh pastries, at a family-friendly bistro.

- Afternoon: Outdoor Adventure in the Loire Valley

Spend your afternoon enjoying the region's natural beauty. Opt for a family-friendly bike ride along the Loire à Vélo, a dedicated cycling route that runs alongside the river. Alternatively, consider a boat trip on the Loire River for a relaxed afternoon exploring the riverbanks and observing local wildlife.

- Evening: Relax in a Loire Valley Village

After your outdoor adventure, relax in one of the Loire's charming villages. Visit Montrichard, a quiet riverside town where you can take a peaceful walk along the banks and enjoy dinner at a local restaurant.

Day 4: Explore the Hidden Gems of the Loire

- Morning: Visit the Village of Candes-Saint-Martin

Head out to explore the picturesque village of Candes-Saint-Martin, one of the most beautiful villages in France. Nestled at the confluence of the Loire and Vienne Rivers, this village is home to cobbled streets, charming stone houses, and incredible views.

- Lunch: Picnic by the River

Enjoy a scenic lunch by the river with fresh ingredients bought at the local market. Relax by the water and watch the boats pass by, enjoying the peaceful ambiance of the village.

- Afternoon: Explore the Troglodyte Dwellings of Rochemenier

Spend the afternoon discovering the fascinating troglodyte dwellings at Rochemenier. This unique site features homes carved into the rock, offering a glimpse into the past and a fun educational experience for children. It's a great spot for the whole family to explore, as well as an off-the-beaten-path experience.

- Evening: Dinner in Saumur

After a full day of exploration, head to Saumur, known for its equestrian culture and stunning château. Enjoy dinner at a local restaurant and take a stroll along the river in the evening.

Day 5: Cultural Immersion and Relaxation

- Morning: Loire Music and Arts Festival

If you're visiting in summer, spend your last day enjoying a local music or arts festival. The Loire Valley is known for its vibrant cultural scene, and you can attend events showcasing classical music, jazz, or local artisans' work.

- Lunch: Traditional Loire Meal

For your final lunch, visit a local restaurant serving traditional Loire cuisine. Try rillettes, goat cheese, and of course, a glass of Loire wine.

- Afternoon: Relaxing River Cruise

In the afternoon, take a relaxing river cruise along the Loire River to soak in the region's beautiful scenery. This is a perfect way to unwind before departing, offering views of the châteaux and lush vineyards from the water.

- Evening: Farewell Dinner in Tours

End your Loire Valley adventure with a farewell dinner in Tours. Enjoy a hearty meal at a restaurant in the city center and toast to your memorable journey through one of France's most enchanting regions.

Ideal for:

- Families looking for a mix of fun, outdoor activities and historical exploration.

- Wine enthusiasts seeking to immerse themselves in the Loire's exceptional wine regions.

- Couples or solo travelers wanting to explore hidden gems and cultural highlights at a relaxed pace.

- History buffs and lovers of French architecture, eager to explore iconic châteaux and charming villages.

This 5-day itinerary allows you to delve deep into the Loire Valley's history, culture, and natural beauty, offering an enriching and well-rounded experience. Whether you're cycling along the Loire River, tasting world-class wines, or exploring fairy-tale castles, you'll leave with lasting memories of one of France's most captivating regions.

CHAPTER 8: Seasonal Events & Festivals

The Loire Valley's cultural calendar is as diverse as the region itself, with a wide variety of seasonal events and festivals celebrating its history, art, food, and, of course, its wines. Whether you're visiting during the vibrant spring bloom, the sun-drenched summer months, or the festive winter season, the Loire offers something special for every traveler. Here's a look at some of the key seasonal events and festivals that are not to be missed.

Spring: A Time for Renewal and Celebration

- Les Renaissances du Château de Blois (May)

Held in May at the Château de Blois, this event celebrates the Renaissance era with performances, music, historical reenactments, and theatrical performances. It's a fantastic way to step back in time and experience the Loire's rich cultural heritage. Families and history enthusiasts alike will find this event immersive and educational.

- **Festival of Flowers in Tours (April-May)**

Spring in the Loire is marked by the Festival of Flowers in Tours, where the city comes alive with vibrant floral displays. This festival includes flower markets, garden exhibitions, and floral art installations throughout the city, making it the perfect event for those who love gardens and nature. You can also take guided tours through the town's beautiful green spaces.

- **Loire Valley Wine Fair (Late Spring)**

Held annually in Saumur or Angers, the Loire Valley Wine Fair (Foire aux Vins de Loire) is an essential event for wine lovers. With over 300 producers showcasing the best wines from the region, including Vouvray, Chinon, and Sancerre, this event provides the perfect opportunity to taste the Loire's finest offerings. Attendees can enjoy tastings, masterclasses, and wine-themed workshops.

Summer: Festivals, Music, and Outdoor Fun

- **Festival d'Anjou (June-July)**

The Festival d'Anjou is a renowned theater festival that takes place in various historic venues throughout the region. Held in the towns of Angers and Saumur, this festival features outdoor performances, often in château courtyards, where plays and operas are brought to life in a beautiful, historic setting. The open-air performances against the backdrop of centuries-old castles make this a unique cultural experience.

- **Touraine Wine Festival (July)**

The Touraine Wine Festival is one of the Loire's top events, showcasing the wine culture of the region. Held in Tours, the festival features wine tastings, local food pairings, and live music. Visitors can mingle with producers and explore the diverse wine varieties of the Loire Valley, including the famous Côteaux du Layon and Touraine Sauvignon.

- **La Fête de la Musique (June 21st)**

Every year, on June 21st, the Fête de la Musique fills the streets of the Loire Valley with music in celebration of the summer solstice. Artists of all genres perform on outdoor stages, from jazz and classical to rock and folk. In cities like Tours, Angers, and Saumur, you'll find lively performances in parks, town squares, and along the riverside. It's a perfect evening for those who enjoy live music and a festive atmosphere.

Autumn: Harvest Celebrations and Scenic Beauty

- **Fête des Vendanges (Harvest Festival) in Montargis (September)**

Autumn in the Loire Valley is synonymous with the harvest season, and the Fête des Vendanges is one of the most important celebrations. Held in the village of Montargis, this festival honors the region's wine harvest with parades, wine tastings, live music, and vibrant markets. This event is especially popular among wine enthusiasts, as it gives a deep dive into the region's winemaking culture.

- **Les Promenades Gourmandes (September)**

For foodies, Les Promenades Gourmandes in Tours is a not-to-miss event. It's a gastronomic tour that lets you sample local specialties, such as rillettes, Tarte Tatin, and of course, Loire wines. Local chefs and producers showcase their culinary creations, giving you a taste of the Loire's best seasonal ingredients.

- **Autumn Wine Tasting Events (September-November)**

Autumn is a prime time to explore the Loire's vineyards during the harvest period. Many of the region's wine estates host private tours, tastings, and harvest celebrations, offering visitors a chance to participate in the winemaking process, sample fresh wine, and learn about the art of wine production. Vineyards in Sancerre, Vouvray, and Chinon all host special events to celebrate the harvest season.

Winter: Festive Markets and Holiday Charm

- **Christmas Markets in Tours and Angers (December)**

The Loire Valley's Christmas markets are a magical way to experience the region during the winter months. Both Tours and Angers host charming markets with festive lights, locally crafted goods, delicious seasonal treats, and mulled wine. The Place du Palais de Justice in Tours becomes a winter wonderland, filled with artisan stalls offering handcrafted gifts and regional delicacies.

- **La Saint-Sylvestre (New Year's Eve in Saumur)**

Saumur celebrates New Year's Eve with a bang, featuring a festive outdoor event in the town square, where locals and visitors gather to watch fireworks and enjoy a night of revelry. It's the perfect way to say goodbye to the year and usher in the next with the beauty of the Loire's historic surroundings.

Year-Round Events: A Celebration of Loire's Heritage

- **Les Châteaux en Fête (Châteaux Festival)**

Held year-round at various châteaux throughout the Loire Valley, Les Châteaux en Fête offers cultural performances, exhibitions, and themed events. Each château adds its unique twist to the celebration, from medieval jousts at Château de Langeais to art exhibits at Château de Chenonceau. These events provide a continuous celebration of the Loire's history and royal past.

- **Loire Valley Arts and Crafts Exhibitions**

Many of the Loire's towns, such as Saumur and Chinon, host regular arts and crafts exhibitions. Whether you're an art lover or just interested in local crafts, these events showcase the talents of regional artists and artisans. From paintings and pottery to woodwork and textiles, the exhibitions provide insight into the Loire Valley's vibrant creative scene.

When to Visit

Each season in the Loire Valley offers unique experiences. Whether you're in search of spring blooms, summer festivals, autumn harvest celebrations, or winter charm, the Loire has something to offer year-round. For wine lovers, harvest season is particularly rewarding, while families may enjoy the summer festivals or spring flower events. Winter markets create a festive atmosphere perfect for holiday travelers, while the warmer months are great for exploring the vineyards and enjoying outdoor activities.

Whichever season you choose to visit, the Loire's rich cultural landscape will make your trip unforgettable.

CHAPTER 9: TRAVEL ETIQUETTE AND LOCAL INSIGHTS

The Loire Valley is a region steeped in history, culture, and natural beauty. As a visitor, respecting local customs, historical sites, and natural areas ensures that your presence is appreciated and helps preserve the region's treasures for future generations. Here's what you should know to be a considerate traveler in this enchanting region.

Respecting Historical Sites and Monuments

The Loire Valley is home to many châteaux, medieval villages, and UNESCO World Heritage Sites that draw visitors from around the world. These places are not just attractions—they are pieces of history, often holding deep cultural and architectural significance. Here's how to make your visit respectful:

• Observe Opening Hours and Rules: Many of the Loire's historical sites, including the famous Château de Chambord and Château de Chenonceau, have specific visiting hours and rules. Be sure to check ahead for opening times, and always follow posted guidelines once you arrive. For example, some châteaux may restrict photography in certain areas or require silence in sensitive rooms.

• Do Not Touch Artifacts or Displays: When visiting museums or historical buildings, refrain from touching exhibits, statues, or artworks. The oils and dirt on your hands can cause irreparable damage to delicate pieces. Many sites have signs indicating where photos are allowed, so always ask if you're unsure.

• Minimize Noise: Many of the Loire's sites have an atmosphere of tranquility, from the quiet gardens at Château de Villandry to the serene halls of Château d'Azay-le-Rideau. Keep noise to a minimum—especially in areas where other visitors are enjoying the peaceful surroundings. Speak in hushed tones and be mindful of your surroundings.

• Guided Tours: If possible, join a guided tour to learn about the history and significance of the place you are visiting. Local guides are often passionate about the region's heritage and can provide fascinating insights that make your experience even more enriching.

Respecting Natural Areas

The Loire Valley is blessed with vast, unspoiled natural landscapes, from its tranquil riversides to the lush vineyards and rolling hills. The region's commitment to preserving its natural beauty is evident, and visitors are encouraged to help protect the environment by following a few basic guidelines:

• Stay on Marked Trails: If you're exploring natural parks like Parc Naturel Régional Loire-Anjou-Touraine or enjoying the cycling paths along the Loire à Vélo, always stick to marked trails. Venturing off-path can damage fragile ecosystems and disturb wildlife.

• Leave No Trace: Whether you're hiking, cycling, or enjoying a leisurely picnic in the countryside, make sure to leave no trace behind. Bring a bag to collect your trash and dispose of it properly. The Loire is famous for its pristine natural beauty, and maintaining this requires the care of every visitor.

• Respect Wildlife: The Loire Valley is home to a variety of wildlife, including birds, deer, and wild boar. Keep a respectful distance from animals and avoid disturbing them. Never feed animals, as it can interfere with their natural behavior.

• Support Sustainable Tourism: Choose eco-friendly activities whenever possible. Many vineyards in the Loire are now adopting sustainable farming practices, and several tour operators offer eco-conscious experiences, like electric bike rentals or organic wine tours. Opting for these experiences ensures that your travel footprint is lighter.

General Local Etiquette

In addition to respecting historical and natural sites, there are a few general etiquette tips that will help you blend in with the local culture and make your visit even more enjoyable:

- **Politeness is Key:** French culture values politeness, especially in interactions with locals. Always greet people with a "Bonjour" (Good day) or "Bonsoir" (Good evening) when entering shops or cafes. A simple "Merci" (Thank you) goes a long way as well. If you're unsure about something, "Excusez-moi" (Excuse me) is always a good start.

- **Dress Modestly:** While the Loire Valley is not as formal as Paris, dressing neatly and modestly is appreciated, especially when visiting religious sites or formal settings. For example, when visiting churches or certain châteaux, you may be asked to cover your shoulders or remove hats.

- **Dining Etiquette:** If you're dining at a local café or restaurant, wait to be seated rather than just walking up to a table. In most places, it's customary to wait for the server's invitation. It's also polite to wait until everyone has been served before starting your meal. And remember, tipping is not mandatory in France, but it's common to leave a small amount (5-10%) for good service.

- **Timing is Everything:** While the French are not overly rigid about time, it's good form to be on time for appointments, tours, or events. Punctuality is especially important for wine tastings or guided tours, where the schedule often runs on a strict timetable.

Engaging with Local Culture

The Loire Valley is full of cultural experiences that are unique to the region, from local markets in Tours and Saumur to traditional festivals. When attending such events or visiting small towns, here's how to be a considerate guest:

- **Support Local Producers:** Whether you're shopping at a market, attending a wine tasting, or dining at a local restaurant, try to support the region's artisans and producers. Crottin de Chavignol (goat cheese) and local wines like Sancerre and Vouvray are famous for their quality, and your purchases help keep local traditions alive.

- **Participate in Festivals with Respect:** Festivals in the Loire often have deep cultural and historical significance. When attending, be sure to understand the customs or dress codes if they exist. For example, in medieval festivals like Les Renaissances du Château de Blois, wearing period costumes or respecting the formalities of the event adds to the fun and shows respect for the traditions.

- **Learn Some Basic French:** While many people in the Loire Valley speak English, learning a few basic French phrases can go a long way in building rapport with locals. Simple phrases like "Où est…" (Where is…), "Combien ça coûte ?" (How much does it cost?), and

"Pouvez-vous m'aider ?" (Can you help me?) will be appreciated and can enrich your experience.

Conclusion

By following these travel etiquette guidelines and respecting the local culture, you'll not only enjoy a richer experience in the Loire Valley, but you'll also help preserve the beauty and history of the region for future generations of travelers. Whether you're exploring a château, cycling along the river, or dining at a local café, always remember that respectful behavior goes hand in hand with unforgettable travel experiences.

Cultural Tips for Interacting with Locals in the Loire Valley

The Loire Valley is a region that prides itself on its rich history, warm hospitality, and a slower pace of life. While the locals are generally welcoming, understanding and respecting French customs can help ensure your interactions are positive and enjoyable. Here are some cultural tips to guide you as you engage with the people of the Loire Valley:

1. Greetings and Politeness

In France, greetings are an essential part of daily life, and the French take politeness seriously. When interacting with locals, always start with a friendly greeting.

• Use Formal Greetings: When entering a shop, café, or any other public space, say "Bonjour" (Good day) or "Bonsoir" (Good evening) depending on the time of day. It's important to acknowledge people when you enter and leave establishments, even if you're just passing by.

- Addressing People: Use "Monsieur" (Mr.) or "Madame" (Mrs.) when speaking to someone, unless they invite you to do otherwise. The use of formal titles is appreciated in most situations.

- Kissing Cheeks: In some regions of France, it's common to greet close friends or family with a light kiss on both cheeks (known as "la bise"). However, this is not always expected from strangers, especially in more formal settings, so it's best to wait for the other person's cues.

2. Respect for Personal Space

French culture values personal space, and the concept of privacy is important. Be mindful of this when engaging with locals.

- Physical Distance: Keep a respectful physical distance when speaking to someone, especially in public spaces. While you might see close friends exchanging a kiss or a hug, this is usually reserved for those who know each other well. In formal or professional settings, a handshake is appropriate.

- Volume of Conversation: The French generally prefer a quieter, more reserved demeanor in public places. Avoid speaking too loudly, especially in quieter or more intimate settings like cafés or local markets.

3. Dining Etiquette

Meals are an important part of French culture, and dining is often viewed as an opportunity for social connection. Understanding the local dining customs will ensure you make a good impression.

• Wait for the Host to Begin: If you're invited to someone's home, it's customary to wait for the host to begin the meal by saying, "Bon appétit" (Enjoy your meal) before you start eating.

• Keep Your Hands Visible: During meals, place your hands on the table (but not your elbows). It's considered impolite to rest your elbows on the table while eating, though keeping your hands visible is a sign of good manners.

• Course by Course: French meals are typically served in multiple courses, and rushing through them can be seen as disrespectful. Take your time, enjoy the meal, and savor each course as it's presented.

4. Tipping and Service

In France, service charges are typically included in your bill (indicated as "service compris"), but tipping is still appreciated for good service, especially in more casual settings.

• In Restaurants: If you receive exceptional service, leaving a small tip (5-10% of the bill) is common, although not mandatory. In cafés or bars, rounding up the bill is also a nice gesture.

- **Tipping in Other Situations:** In taxis or when receiving a guided tour, tipping is optional but appreciated if the service exceeds expectations. A small amount (5-10% of the fare) is typically enough.

5. Conversing in French

While many people in the Loire Valley speak English, making the effort to speak French, even if it's just a few words, will go a long way in building rapport and showing respect for the local culture.

- **Learn Key Phrases:** Start with basics like "Bonjour" (Hello), "Merci" (Thank you), and "S'il vous plaît" (Please). Learning phrases like "Où est…" (Where is…) or "Pouvez-vous m'aider ?" (Can you help me?) can be very useful.

- **Politeness Over Fluency:** The French appreciate when foreigners make an effort, even if your French is not perfect. If you don't speak the language fluently, don't worry—simply trying shows respect. If you need to switch to English, it's usually fine, but always begin with a polite greeting in French.

6. Punctuality

Punctuality is valued in France, but it's important to note that there's a more relaxed attitude to time in some situations, especially in rural areas.

- **Appointments and Tours:** Be on time for any scheduled activities, including tours, train departures, or reservations. For more casual events, like social gatherings, arriving within 15-30 minutes of the agreed time is considered acceptable, but try to avoid being too late.

• **Respecting Time for Meals:** Lunch in France typically occurs from 12:00 to 2:00 PM, and dinner may not begin until after 7:30 PM. Keep these times in mind when planning meals or activities around mealtimes.

7. Respect for Local Traditions

In a region like the Loire Valley, with its rich agricultural history and traditional way of life, respecting local customs and traditions is an important aspect of cultural engagement.

• **Support Local Producers:** The Loire Valley is known for its wine and artisanal food products. When visiting local markets, always ask about where the produce or wine comes from. Showing an interest in local goods is a great way to connect with producers and shop owners.

• **Participating in Local Festivals:** The Loire hosts several unique festivals throughout the year, from wine festivals to medieval reenactments. When participating, be sure to observe the local dress codes, customs, and rules. Engaging respectfully with these celebrations will deepen your understanding of the culture.

8. Engaging with Local Farmers and Artisans

The Loire Valley is home to many small-scale farmers and artisans who take great pride in their work, whether it's producing wine, cheese, or hand-crafted goods. When engaging with them:

• **Ask Questions:** Locals love to talk about their craft, whether it's winemaking or cheese production. Feel free to ask questions, as it shows interest in their work and a respect for their knowledge.

• **Respect for Craftsmanship:** Whether you're purchasing a bottle of wine or a piece of local pottery, be sure to express appreciation for the craftsmanship involved. This will help you build rapport and may lead to further recommendations or insights.

By following these cultural tips for interacting with locals, you'll find that your experience in the Loire Valley becomes more authentic, enriching, and respectful. Showing interest in the local way of life not only deepens your connection to the region, but it also makes you a welcome guest in the Loire's charming towns, vineyards, and villages.

CHAPTER 10: FAQS AND TROUBLESHOOTING FOR THE LOIRE VALLEY

Traveling in the Loire Valley is typically a smooth and enjoyable experience, but it's always good to be prepared for unexpected situations. Below are some common questions and tips on how to handle emergencies, medical concerns, weather issues, and other potential hiccups during your visit.

What should I do in case of a medical emergency in the Loire Valley?

While the Loire Valley is a relatively safe region, it's essential to know what to do in case of an emergency.

- **Emergency Numbers:**

 - For medical emergencies, call 112 (European emergency number) or 15 (ambulance). This number works for all emergencies, including medical, fire, and police.

 - For non-urgent medical matters, you can visit a local pharmacy. Many pharmacies in the Loire Valley have an open-door policy, and pharmacists are often helpful with basic medical advice.

- **Local Hospitals:**

 - The major cities in the Loire Valley, like Tours and Orléans, have hospitals with emergency services. Centre Hospitalier Universitaire de Tours is one of the largest in the region.

 - If you're in a smaller town, you can find the nearest medical center or doctor by asking locals or checking your map app for nearby clinics.

 - Travel Insurance: Always ensure you have travel insurance that covers medical emergencies. This is essential, especially if you're traveling from outside the European Union.

What should I do if I lose my passport or wallet?

Losing important documents can be stressful, but there are steps you can take to resolve the situation.

• Report the Loss: Immediately report the loss to the local police by visiting the nearest police station or calling 17 (French police emergency number). This helps you file a report, which may be needed for your insurance claim or for obtaining replacement documents.

• Contact Your Embassy: If you're a foreign traveler, contact your country's embassy or consulate in France. They can issue emergency travel documents to help you continue your trip.

• Cancel Credit Cards: Call your bank or credit card company to cancel any lost or stolen cards. They may be able to send you a replacement card or assist you with securing funds in the meantime.

What should I do if I have trouble with public transportation?

• Trains and Buses: If you have issues with train or bus services, such as delays or cancellations, check the schedule updates on platforms like SNCF (France's national train service) or Rémi (regional buses in the Loire Valley). Staff at the train station or bus stop are often bilingual and can help guide you.

• Taxis or Ride-Sharing: In case of problems with taxis or ride-sharing services like Uber, you can always contact the service provider through their app or customer service numbers. In case of disputes or issues with the ride, ask for a receipt or documentation to address the issue later.

• Lost Luggage: If your luggage is lost during a train journey, report it to the SNCF baggage services immediately. They'll assist in tracking your luggage and will usually help you with a claim for delayed or lost items.

What should I do if there's bad weather during my visit?

The Loire Valley experiences a range of weather conditions depending on the season, but sudden weather changes can occasionally disrupt plans.

• Rain: If it rains, especially during spring or autumn, it's a good idea to carry an umbrella or wear a waterproof jacket. Many of the Loire's attractions, like its vineyards and châteaux, have covered areas or indoor spaces to explore if the weather is unfavorable.

• Flooding: Though rare, flooding can occur along the Loire River during heavy rain. Always monitor local news or weather apps for warnings. If you're near the river, follow local authorities' guidelines and avoid areas that are marked as dangerous.

• Heatwaves: Summers in the Loire can be warm, and heatwaves can sometimes cause discomfort.

Stay hydrated, wear a hat, sunscreen, and light clothing. Avoid outdoor activities during the peak midday heat and take advantage of indoor attractions, such as museums and châteaux, during the hottest hours.

What should I do if I don't speak French and have trouble communicating?

While many people in the Loire Valley speak at least some English, not everyone will be fluent. Here are some tips to make communication easier:

• Learn Key Phrases: Even if you don't speak French, learning a few key phrases can go a long way in making locals more receptive. Simple phrases like "Bonjour" (Hello), "Merci" (Thank you), and "Parlez-vous anglais?" (Do you speak English?) are good starters.

• Translation Apps: Download a translation app like Google Translate. It can help in restaurants, shops, and with directions, especially in rural areas where English may be less commonly spoken.

• Use Gestures: The French understand body language. If you're struggling to communicate, don't hesitate to use hand gestures to explain what you need. This often works, particularly in more rural settings.

What should I do if I miss an event or activity I had planned?

If you've missed a specific event, such as a vineyard tour or a cultural festival, don't panic—there are usually plenty of alternative options available.

- **Check for Alternatives:** If you've missed a vineyard tour, many wineries in the Loire Valley offer drop-in tastings or tours throughout the day. Ask local businesses, hotels, or tourist information centers if there are other available tours or events in the area.

- **Look for Nearby Events:** Check apps like Eventbrite or Visit Loire Valley to find any last-minute festivals, exhibitions, or performances that you can attend instead.

What should I do if I'm feeling unsafe?

The Loire Valley is a relatively safe region, but like anywhere else, it's important to stay aware of your surroundings.

- **Stay in Well-Lit Areas:** If you're walking in the evening, try to stay in well-lit, populated areas. Avoid walking alone in isolated places late at night.

- **Emergency Assistance:** If you feel unsafe or need assistance, call the local police at 17 or visit a nearby shop or café where locals can help guide you to a safer location.

Being prepared for the unexpected is essential when traveling, and knowing what to do in case of emergencies or minor setbacks can help you enjoy your time in the Loire Valley with peace of mind. Keep important contact numbers, insurance details, and emergency protocols on hand so you're ready for anything during your trip.

How to Handle Language Barriers Effectively in the Loire Valley

While many people in the Loire Valley, particularly in larger cities and tourist spots, speak some level of English, not everyone will be fluent. In rural areas or smaller towns, French is the dominant language. Here are some tips to effectively navigate language barriers during your trip.

1. Learn a Few Key Phrases

Even if you don't speak French fluently, knowing a few essential phrases can make a big difference. Locals appreciate when visitors try to communicate in their language, even if it's just for politeness.

- Basic Greetings and Phrases:
- Bonjour (Hello)
- Merci (Thank you)
- Excusez-moi, parlez-vous anglais ? (Excuse me, do you speak English?)

- Combien ça coûte ? (How much does it cost?)

- Où est… ? (Where is…?)

- Je ne parle pas bien français. (I don't speak French very well.)

- Pouvez-vous m'aider ? (Can you help me?)

Even these few phrases will often help you establish rapport and show that you're making an effort.

2. Use a Translation App

In today's digital age, language translation apps are incredibly helpful and easy to use. Apps like Google Translate or iTranslate can help translate text, speech, and even images (like signs or menus).

- Offline Mode: Download your chosen translation app before your trip to ensure you can use it even without a Wi-Fi connection, especially in rural areas where internet access may be limited.

- Voice Input: Most apps allow you to speak into your phone, and they'll translate your words into French. This is particularly useful when ordering food or asking for directions.

3. Non-Verbal Communication

When words fail, gestures and body language can go a long way. People generally understand basic hand signals, such as pointing to indicate directions or using universal gestures like holding your hand to your stomach to show you're hungry.

- Pointing: If you're looking for something specific (a shop, restaurant, or landmark), you can point to a map or a picture. You can also show an address or phone number to make your request clearer.

- Polite Gestures: In France, politeness is important. A warm smile and a friendly attitude can help ease any tension when there's a language gap.

4. Stay Patient and Use Simple Language

It's important to be patient with both yourself and the locals. If you don't speak French fluently, try to speak slowly and clearly, and avoid complicated sentences. Simple and direct questions are often more effective.

- Simplify Your Questions: Rather than asking long, complex questions, break them down into shorter, clearer ones. For example, instead of asking, "Where can I find a good restaurant with vegetarian options near the château?" you could ask, "Where is a restaurant?" or "Do you have vegetarian food?"

- Use English for Common Travel Words: Certain travel-related words (e.g., hotel, bus, taxi, airport) are often understood in English, even in rural areas.

5. Be Mindful of Cultural Differences

While a language barrier can create challenges, it's important to remember that cultural differences also play a role in communication. In France, people value courtesy, so always start with a polite greeting (e.g., Bonjour), and avoid immediately switching to English without first attempting French.

- Respect for Personal Space: French people typically value their personal space more than in some other cultures. Maintain a respectful distance when speaking and avoid speaking too loudly.

- Body Language: Keep in mind that in France, it's common to use subtle hand gestures when speaking. You can adapt by being mindful of your own gestures, but don't worry too much—just follow the lead of those around you.

6. Ask for Help from Younger Locals or Tourism Services

Many younger French people, especially in urban and tourist-friendly areas, speak English better than older generations. If you're in a situation where communication is difficult, try asking younger locals or students for help.

- Tourist Information Centers: If you're struggling to communicate, visiting a tourist office can be a great solution. Staff there are typically fluent in English and can help with directions, booking tickets, and giving recommendations.

- Hotel Staff: Most hotel staff in the Loire Valley are accustomed to dealing with international travelers, so they can often help with translation or answer questions in English.

7. Use Visual Aids and Maps

When words fall short, visual aids can be extremely helpful. Keep a map of the region with you and highlight places or routes. If you need to explain something, showing the location on a map can bridge the language gap effectively.

• Menus: In restaurants, many will have menus with pictures or at least a few English words for tourists. If there's no English translation available, don't hesitate to use your app to translate the menu or ask your waiter for help.

• Signs and Symbols: Look for international symbols, especially in places like museums, train stations, or airports. These visual clues can guide you when language fails.

8. Stay Calm and Have a Sense of Humor

Language barriers can be frustrating, but maintaining a calm and positive attitude will help both you and the people you're interacting with feel more at ease. A smile, a simple "désolé" (sorry), and a willingness to make light of the situation can go a long way.

• Humor: Sometimes, humor can transcend language barriers. If something goes wrong, don't be afraid to laugh at yourself. It shows that you're not taking yourself too seriously and that you're trying your best.

Navigating language barriers in the Loire Valley can be challenging, but with patience, a few key phrases, and some helpful tools, you can still enjoy a seamless and rewarding experience. Remember, the effort you make to speak French will often be appreciated, and the French are generally understanding when it comes to tourists trying to communicate.

FINAL WORDS

As your journey through the Loire Valley draws to a close, take a moment to appreciate the beauty, tranquility, and timeless charm of this remarkable region. The Loire offers more than just its famous châteaux and vineyards; it provides an experience that slows down time, inviting you to immerse yourself fully in its rhythm. Whether you're wandering through the cobblestone streets of a medieval town, savoring a glass of Vouvray wine, or admiring the reflection of a château in the calm river waters, the Loire captures the essence of French elegance and simplicity.

In the fast-paced world we live in, the Loire encourages you to embrace a slower, more deliberate pace. It's a place where you can pause and appreciate the finer things—whether that's the beauty of nature, the joy of sharing a meal with loved ones, or the serenity of a peaceful afternoon. Don't rush through your visit; instead, savor each moment. Take the time to explore the hidden corners of the region, chat with locals, and fully absorb the sights, sounds, and flavors of this enchanting destination.

Above all, remember that the Loire is not just a place on the map—it's a living, breathing region full of stories, traditions, and experiences waiting to be discovered. So go ahead, step off the beaten path, and allow the Loire's charm to sweep you away. Your adventure here may end, but the memories of its beauty, warmth, and spirit will linger long after you've left. Safe travels and may the Loire remain in your heart as a place of timeless magic.

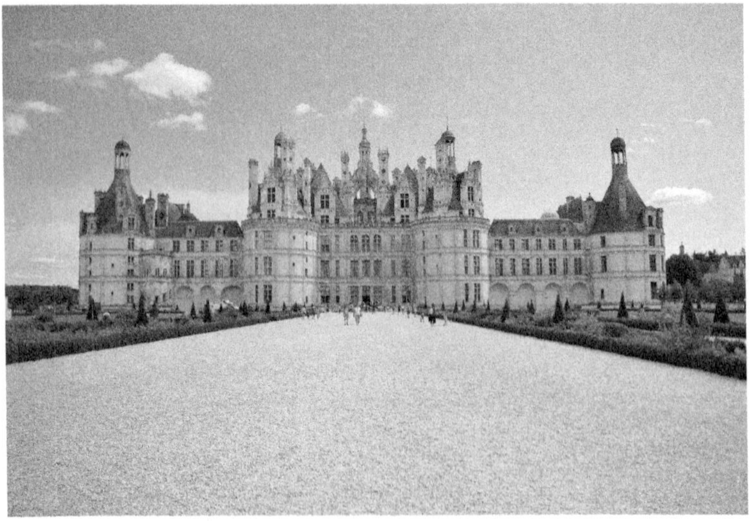

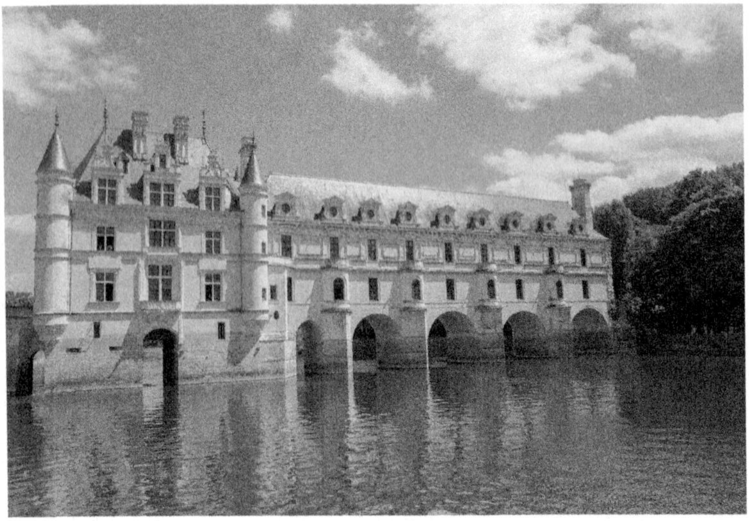

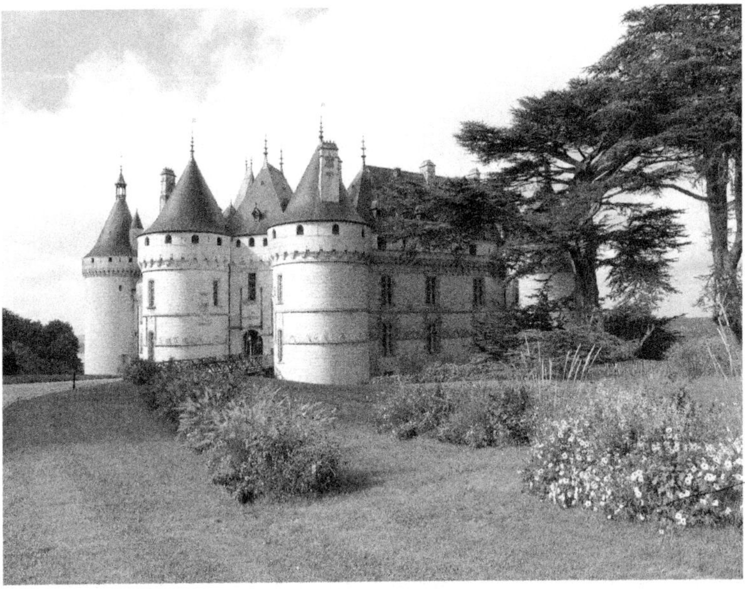

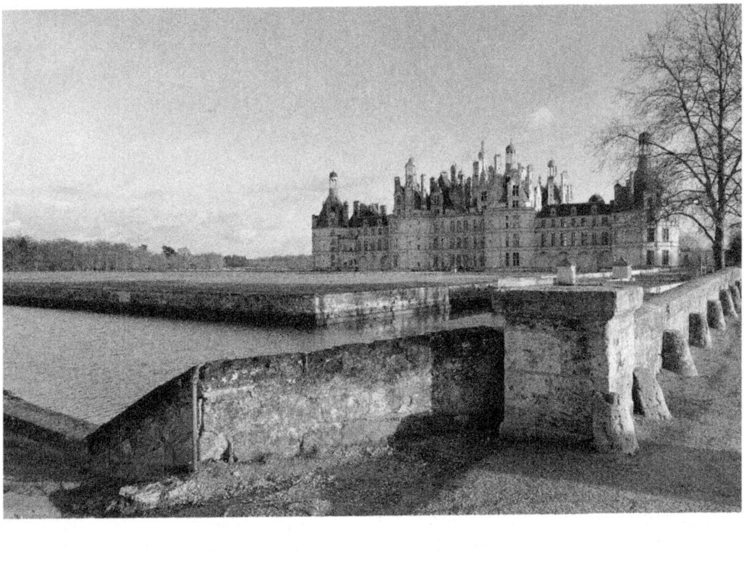

GET ACCESS TO MORE BOOKS BY THE AUTHOR

Printed in Dunstable, United Kingdom